Joycee Kennedy
Carol J. McCarthy

Bridging Worlds
Understanding and Facilitating Adolescent Recovery from the Trauma of Abuse

*Pre-publication
REVIEWS,
COMMENTARIES,
EVALUATIONS . . .*

"**B***ridging Worlds* focuses the attention of the reader on the real teenager. It provides a paradigm shift from seeing an abused child as a victim to recognizing the heroism in that teen's coping. Kennedy and McCarthy have helped define heroic coping styles and provided help to people who work with teens who have been abused. I hope that foster parents, people working in social services, clinicians, and therapists have the opportunity to read this work.

They will find it a beacon of light and support in what otherwise is a morass of re-traumatizing, categorizing, dehumanizing jargon. The vignettes are moving and powerful. Teenagers as well as society at large would benefit if the CASTT model were replicated in other settings. To shift an approach to a traumatized teen from pity to awe is a significant accomplishment for the authors to have facilitated and defined."

David I. Berland, MD
*Clinical Professor,
Former Director,
Division of Child and Adolescent
Psychiatry, St. Louis University
School of Medicine,
St. Louis, MO*

"The authors have given us an extraordinary survey of the history of child neglect and abuse in America, juxtaposing our national priorities of the humane care of animals, the aged, and the environment before that of children. The societal challenge they place before us as mental health professionals is to find the will to stem the hemorrhaging of our traumatized youth into psychosis or the criminal justice system.

Reframing existing mental health theory and educational and institutional care would appear to be their intent. Rather than viewing the taking of case history as a cursory introduction to diagnosing youngsters, the authors view it not only as the source of the etiology but as part of the repair of the child's personal and world view. As in a detective story, the pieces of the child's puzzle are needed to grasp the depth of the trauma that the child must find a way to integrate with self-respect. Thus, while making the assessment for PTSD, rather than the other personality disorders, clarification may be brought to the strategies that will be needed by the child.

This book will be a wonderful teaching tool at the university level but should be required reading in high schools as well."

Florabel Kinsler, PhD
Licensed Clinical Social Worker;
Board-certified Diplomate,
Los Angeles, CA

HMTP

The Haworth Maltreatment and Trauma Press
An Imprint of The Haworth Press, Inc.

Bridging Worlds
Understanding and Facilitating
Adolescent Recovery
from the Trauma of Abuse

THE HAWORTH MALTREATMENT & TRAUMA PRESS
Robert A. Geffner, PhD
Editor

New, Recent, and Forthcoming Titles:

Sexual, Physical, and Emotional Abuse in Out-of-Home Care: Prevention Skills for At-Risk Children by Toni Cavanagh Johnson and Associates

Cedar House: A Model Child Abuse Treatment Program by Bobbi Kendig with Clara Lowry

Bridging Worlds: Understanding and Facilitating Adolescent Recovery from the Trauma of Abuse by Joycee Kennedy and Carol McCarthy

The Learning About Myself (LAMS) Program for At-Risk Parents: Learning from the Past—Changing the Future by Verna Rickard

The Learning About Myself (LAMS) Handbook for Group Participants by Verna Rickard

Treating Children with Sexually Abusive Behavior Problems: Guidelines for Child and Parent Intervention by Jan Ellen Burton, Lucinda A. Rasmussen, Julie Bradshaw, Barbara J. Christopherson, and Steven C. Huke

Bridging Worlds
Understanding and Facilitating Adolescent Recovery from the Trauma of Abuse

Joycee Kennedy
Carol J. McCarthy

The Haworth Maltreatment and Trauma Press
An Imprint of The Haworth Press, Inc.
New York • London

Published by

The Haworth Maltreatment & Trauma Press, an imprint of The Haworth Press, Inc., 10 Alice Street, Binghamton, NY 13904-1580

Chapter 5 quotes material from *Savage Inequalities* by Jonathan Kozol. Copyright © 1991 by Jonathan Kozol. Reprinted by permission of Crown Publishers, Inc.

Chapter 6 quotes material from *A Separate Peace* by John Knowles. Copyright © 1959 by John Knowles. Reprinted by permission of Curtis Brown, Ltd.

Cover design by Marylouise E. Doyle.

Library of Congress Cataloging-in-Publication Data

Kennedy, Joycee.
   Bridging worlds : understanding and facilitating adolescent recovery from the trauma of abuse / Joycee Kennedy, Carol J. McCarthy.
       p.   cm.
   Includes bibliographical references and index.
   ISBN 0-7890-0089-X (alk. paper).
   1. Abused teenagers.   2. Adolescent psychotherapy.   3. Problem youth—Rehabilitation.
I. McCarthy, Carol J. II. Title.
RJ507.A29K46 1998
616.85'8223'00835—dc21   97-37274
                                                                                    CIP

This book is written in praise of young people
who have survived the trauma of child abuse.

Those of us who take vows as mental health workers
need to give a face and a voice to those who have suffered.

ABOUT THE AUTHORS

Joycee Kennedy, LCSW, BCD, has been a therapist with the Aurora Mental Health Center in Colorado for nearly twenty years. She specializes in the treatment of children and adolescents with traumatic stress from child abuse. For nine years, she was the Director of Hampden Academy, an adolescent day treatment program of the Aurora Mental Health Center team that was awarded a half-million dollar research grant and an educational video grant. She is contributing writer to Beverly James' book about trauma and attachment in childhood. Ms. Kennedy earned her BA degree with high honors, Phi Beta Kappa, from the University of Connecticut in 1973 and received her MSW from the University of Denver in 1978.

Carol J. McCarthy, LCSW, has worked in community mental health in various capacities for ten years. Before completing her graduate training, she worked for seven years with survivors of sexual, physical, and emotional abuse in rape crisis counseling, a battered women's shelter, and intensive self-defense courses. Most recently, she developed and implemented a program for adolescents who are at high risk of long-term, out-of-home placement through juvenile justice, child protection, and/or mental health. Ms. McCarthy received her master of social work degree from Smith College School for Social Work in 1992. She currently works in private practice and consultation.

CONTENTS

Foreword

Cameras slowly close in on the familiar haggard face of the fifty-year-old hostage. Released a month ago, he refused to be interviewed until now. Pictures of the hero's return, his family, his childhood, and his hometown saturated the media. There were interviews with government representatives, trauma experts, friends, and neighbors endlessly speculating about his possible isolation and brainwashing, as well as physical, sexual, and emotional torture. The public's appetite was whetted. They hungered for news, for details of the horror and how he survived. The correspondent softly said, "I know I am speaking for the men, women, and children around the country who admire the courage of you and your family. Can you tell us what happened?"

Silence. The hero mouthed something without sound. As the interviewer smoothly covered, he continued haltingly, "Everyone has been kind to me . . . and to my family. I'm sorry. I'm sorry I can't talk about what was done to me . . . the humiliation, the pain . . . not now. I want to tell you a part, a small part of the story. I . . . need help."

The following pause was electric. Our hero, choking back tears, told a stunned audience how his dog had been with him throughout his ordeal. No one had reported this. "They hurt him in ways you would not believe . . . made me watch. We escaped together . . . and I don't think I would have made it without him. The experts, those people won't listen.

"They're afraid of him. They say he's too dangerous . . . that . . . that he is an attack dog and can't learn to be different. He's . . . not a rat in one of their cages. . . . They don't understand he has a heart. Can't he be a hero too? My God," he said in a strangled whisper, "They have so many experts, they could at least. . . . They won't even let me try! . . . You . . . you don't know what being locked up does to him!"

The cameras cut away to the news commentator. Across the country, people respond by phones, faxes, and e-mail to the call for help, to advocate for the violent dog with the heart of a hero.

This is not a true story, unlike the other vignettes in this book, but I believe the reader knows it could be. And it is easy to project further the sincere, passionate public response that would occur—for a dog. A "real" dog with a name, a story, and someone who can be his voice.

Adolescents who have survived horrific experiences in their homes and communities are referred to as heroes by the authors, Joycee Kennedy and Carol J. McCarthy. Why do we, as a wealthy, developed nation with abundant resources, avoid acknowledging the suffering and injustice our youths have survived and, instead, exclusively focus on their disturbing behavior? The answer is bigger than a sound byte. The question compels us to face painful realities, urges us to think deeply about our policies and the treatment of these youths, brings us to recognize our communities' ignorance and shameful neglect of our teenagers abused by family members and public systems. When referring to community systems, "We have met the enemy and they is us" (quote attributed to Pogo).

Adolescents are big; take risks; don't mind; smell and look funny; do things we don't understand; try on various moods, costumes, values, behaviors—sometimes the changes are hourly; they need us and tell us to leave them alone; avoid adults and hang together in groups; rage and hide their vulnerabilities; have problems we cannot relate to; sometimes know more than we do; and—those are the average ones! Traumatized teenagers do all of the above with more intensity and persistence. They alarm and confuse most adults. We often respond to what scares us with anger, distancing, or ignoring. We are frightened because we don't know what to do about their violence, their pain, their silence, their bravado. Just as the dog-with-a-heart in the above vignette, we focus on controlling their behavior and avoid dealing with their suffering, courage, and creativity.

In modern times, the large numbers of traumatized combat veterans and violently assaulted women have led us to recognize, understand, and develop treatment programs for the persistent and profound impact of post-traumatic stress disorder. To illustrate how far we have advanced in our treatment of traumatic stress, during World War I, a soldier in battle, exhibiting what we now know to be symptoms of acute traumatic stress, could be found guilty of treason and shot.

More recently we have begun to recognize traumatized infants, toddlers, and children. Based upon trauma research and clinical experience, specific treatment programs have been developed. Now it is time to address the suffering and symptoms of our adolescents who have been traumatized by abuse and violence. The unique developmental needs, strengths, and vulnerabilities of adolescents often disguise trauma symptoms and also add to the complexities of treatment needs and effective interventions.

Traumatizing environments and events can have a negative impact upon the cognitive, emotional, behavioral, physical, spiritual, and moral development of a still-growing youth. Traumatic stress can affect a youth's learning, health, relationships with others, and way of viewing himself or herself and the world. Since the impact is felt in all these arenas, there, too, must be the focus of healing. There's much more to attend to than the behavior we find frightening and troublesome.

Our traumatized teens, like everyone else, need a safe base from which they can learn to cope with their reality, learn to manage their feelings and behaviors, and figure out who they are separate from their adaptive behavior and protective armor. They need the stability and consistency of a safe place long enough to not only integrate all of their work, but also to develop a sense of belonging and future.

What about resilience? Of course, there are varying degrees of resilience in all human beings, but resilience does not mean a person is unaffected. Abused adolescents still need and deserve our help even though they appear to be coping, and have less noticeable scars. But what if they won't talk, or say everything's okay, or tell me to f__ off? The reader is in for a treat because these authors explain such responses and provide guidance to those who live and work with these adolescents.

This book is a serious, juicy, comprehensive, research-based, easy-to-read, practical handbook for understanding and helping adolescents traumatized by abuse. Based upon their research, the authors provide descriptions of past social attitudes and policies that influence the present structure and thinking in the areas of child protection, juvenile justice, education, and mental health. This comprehensive foundation is then interwoven with current news examples and current policies which together provide the context needed to understand some of the barriers to creative, integrated solutions. The authors provide specific treatment guidelines based upon nine years' effective work with traumatized adolescents. The work goes significantly beyond the single channel of behavior or of cognitive structuring—it is both comprehensive and contextual. It encompasses mind, heart, and spirit as well as behavior.

Is the work hard? Yes. Complex? Yes. Is it worth it? Of course. In a recent conversation with one of the authors, Joycee Kennedy, she described a young adult as follows:

> There is no doubt in my mind that he could have killed someone when he was an acting-out adolescent. He grew up in violence, was sadistically abused, survived multiple failed foster placements, and was hospitalized numerous times. He had an extraordinary number of diagnoses. Along with the intensive work when he felt safe and connected to his therapist, he developed empathy for the child he once was and then for others. I believe that he is now incapable of hurting anyone unless it was to protect his life.

Hope and respect for the courage of adolescents is pervasive in this book. The authors tell us the unspeakable acts perpetrated upon and witnessed by individual adolescents. In doing so they give them a name, a story, and a voice. Readers are moved beneath and beyond the behaviors of these teens who are destructive to themselves and others. We see them as people with a right to the best care we can afford. And we cannot afford not to give it to them. Good, bad, or ugly, they are our kids, our future, our national treasures.

Thank you, Joycee Kennedy and Carol McCarthy, from the many adolescents you have helped, and from the rest of us who learn from you and pass it on. Aloha nui loa.

Beverly James, LCSW
Author of *Handbook for Treatment
of Attachment-Trauma Problems in Children*

Acknowledgments

This book is written in honor of American adolescents, with whom we have shared love and work. These courageous teenagers have inspired *Bridging Worlds*.

I wish to dedicate my work in this book to my father, to the memory of my mother, and to my older brother, Lew, who taught me the meaning of creativity. I would like to acknowledge my birth children, Cary and Jody, who have lovingly and courageously embraced the complexities of their own blended family. I wish to thank my endearing stepchildren, Kimberly, Dawn, and Kevin, and my beloved foster children, Brandi, David, and Bill. I have a special appreciation for Karen Barge, who lived with our family for three years as an adolescent racial exchange student and went on to college on a music scholarship.

I wish to thank my husband, Richard Jackson, who, despite a heavy workload of his own, became my strongest supporter and early technical advisor. I thank Sue Bronson for encouragement, support, and wonderful editing help. I appreciate my aunts, the late Deborah Copeland and the late Pearl Portnoy, for editing help. I wish to thank my stepmother, Barbara Kay, and my younger brother, Robert, for their consistent support after the death of my mother. I appreciate Asha Mangalik, who gave me her own computer to use for six months, and I wish to thank Ruth Gilbert for her enthusiasm and invaluable research assistance.

Over the past twenty years, I have had the privilege of learning from wonderful teachers: I studied with Jamshed Morenas at the Philadelphia Child Guidance Clinic; with Don Krill at the Graduate School of Social Work, University of Denver; with John Peterson at Hampden Academy, Aurora Mental Health Center; with Henry Coppolillo at the University of Colorado Health Sciences Center; and with Rhonda Miescke of Arapahoe County Social Services. Rhonda's vision and support allowed the treatment model presented in this book to be used in public agencies.

At Aurora Mental Health Center, where I have worked for almost two decades, I wish to thank the Executive Director, Randy Stith, and the two Deputy Directors, Frank Bennett and Ron Markovich. I particularly wish to thank Frank Bennett, my immediate boss for fifteen years, for supporting me "beyond the call of duty." I wish to express appreciation to Deborah Sebring for her commitment to directing the wonderful five-year research project and educational video. Also at Aurora Mental Health Center, I wish to thank Ardis Wolf, Sue Skripko, Athena Lansing, George Gielow, Sarah Neal, and John Troske for their help.

From Hampden Academy, an adolescent day treatment program of the Mental Health Center, I have team members whom I appreciate for providing wonderful support for my ideas: Annette Saunders, Jamie Ammann, Sharon Anderson, Darrell Allen, Chris Irwin, Willy Schier, Marj Ruocco, Eileen Stewart, Heraldine Seiber, Kate Yonce, Jane Westlye, Mike Gorman, Ellen Copper, Jim Stokes, Herb Johnson, Mike McHenry, and Jeff Slaga. These people were willing to listen to adolescents and explore new approaches.

Throughout my lifetime I have had the good fortune to have people who have provided me with supportive, unedited friendship while inspiring my work on this book: Suzanne Green, Greta Lindecrantz, Barbara Mueller, Nancy Burdette, John Eisenbud, Bill Schwartz, Eric Karl, Tim Faust, Maria and Robert Blanck, and Stephen Singular.

I thank Beverly James for her encouragement at the beginning of this project when I had a paucity of local support and was believed to be a heretic, and I thank my co-author, Carol McCarthy, who has provided both the cheerleading and academic skill to bring this book to its best. In addition, I thank Bessel van der Kolk, at Harvard University, who endured my consultations and long-distance phone calls as he gave me the foundation for my thinking.

In conclusion, Carol and I wish to thank Dr. Robert Geffner for his patient editing help. His feedback was invaluable in the completion of this work. We would like to also acknowledge William Palmer, Vice President and Managing Editor of The Haworth Press, Inc., for his support of this project from the beginning.

Joycee Kennedy

Thanks to all the young people and their families with whom I have had the privilege to work. Allowing me into your lives has been an honor—one that is not taken lightly.

Working in Boulder County is also a privilege. The youth-serving agencies, including the local mental health center, juvenile justice programs, social services, and schools have a commitment to working collaboratively in the best interests of our young people. Even though everyone does not always agree, there is a commitment to staying within a process to enhance the delivery of services to high-risk youth and their families. I am appreciative of my colleagues for that commitment.

I have been blessed with incredible mentors, teachers, and supervisors over the years who have supported me in my thoughts and hopes for the future. Special thanks to the late Ronah Brodkin, and to Vanessa Kelly, Laura Glassmeyer, Janet Dean, Sue Weatherley, Kathy Pinson, Cindy Silvis, Jim Drisko, Joyce Everett, Carol Corkey, and Phoebe Norton. Thanks also to Joycee Kennedy for taking me on this wild ride through the process of writing and publishing a book. She invited a co-author into this project after working solo on it for several years. Her welcome and openness to the process is appreciated.

Finally, I would like to thank my family of choice and creation, including Michelle David, Gale Stromberg, Connie Peate, Sharri Carson, Corky Carson, Patti Bowen, Karla Rikansrud, Monte Atkinson, P. Diane Wild, Ellen Greenhouse, Lester Wall, Catherine Schieve, Jerry Jacob, and Jamie Ammann. Without each of you, I would not be who I am today. Most especially, thanks to my life partner, Laurie Friedman, who has taught me new definitions of family, trust, and connectedness.

Carol J. McCarthy

Introduction

- A woman was fatally stabbed by her estranged lover. Her seventeen-year-old pregnant daughter fought unsuccessfully to save her. The daughter was also impaled upon the seven-inch weapon. The blade missed the fetus by inches.

- A nineteen-year-old young man entered the Job Corps shortly after being reunited with his mother following a four-year absence. At fourteen, he took drugs, fought, and roamed the streets. For four years he lived in group homes, foster homes, and psychiatric hospitals. At the age of six, he watched his father attempt to murder his mother. He recently stated, "I bet even now, if you cross my father, he will slit your throat."

- A father threw his two-year-old son from a two-story window into a swimming pool and left him to drown. His older brother pulled him safely to the poolside. At age four, this young child witnessed his father murder his mother while he hid frozen in fright under the living room couch.

- A seven-year-old was left by her parents in California to spend the summer months with her grandparents. She spent the next six summers in a rural setting on almost ten acres of California coastline. During those six summers, this young child was sexually penetrated and orally raped weekly by her grandfather.

These are examples of the ways in which adults have abused children. All too often, such experiences are kept hidden inside the minds and hearts of young children. When well-intentioned adults are made aware of such trauma, their responses may be either healing or retraumatizing. When such wounds are left unnoticed, unattended, and unhealed, the impact of the trauma is greatly compounded.

While many abused youths have a level of resilience that enables them to survive child abuse without subsequent dangerous behavior toward self or others, the stories listed above frequently transform into newspaper headlines announcing troubles experienced by adolescents. Out-of-control adolescents have received extensive media coverage in recent years. Teen pregnancy, HIV transmission, gang violence, weapon possession, substance abuse, and school drop-out rates are examples of the difficulties facing youths today. Authors of social policy struggle with these issues as well, as they attempt to intervene on a community level. Stories of the victimization and perpetration of violence among adolescents seem unending. The sheer numbers of youths directly and indirectly exposed to various forms of violence imply that such problems are not individual issues. This has become a major social phenomenon at this time in history.

Deviant behavior is not solely the responsibility of troubled teens. Adolescents are reflections of the adult role models in their lives. Throughout recent history, teens have acted in ways that adults tend to find uncomfortable. Yet, the role of adults is to respond in a helpful way. The prevalent social systems established in this country, such as families, schools, child protection, mental health, and juvenile justice, have responded largely out of a sense of helplessness. Societal responses to out-of-control adolescent behavior are often reactionary, lacking in a long-term vision promoting positive change.

Families frequently turn to social systems for support in handling difficult teens. School systems often fail to differentiate these troubled youths from those of healthy backgrounds, expecting them to be able to concentrate on academic pursuits. Some teenagers are being raised in the child protective system by being moved among placements with various levels of care, often with their possessions in garbage bags. Residential treatment facilities, foster homes, group homes, shelters, and other youth placements often force child protection to remove a child from their care because of the young person's behavior. Inaccurate mental health labels have been attached to some of the most troubled, yet courageous young people. Judicial systems have responded in punitive ways without carefully assessing the psychosocial issues. Oftentimes, adults expect adolescents to have the maturity to discuss their pain rather than act upon it. Through all of these problems, adults have continued to misunderstand the youths by implying that the youths themselves are failures.

Participation in an undeclared social war has become a milestone of the enculturation of America's young throughout the last quarter of the twentieth century. The words and actions of many teenagers are not soft, gentle, or kind. Many of their music lyrics are harsh and abusive. Buildings in major cities are branded by graffiti. The young people are speaking to adults and social institutions through such means. It is the challenge of adults to listen beyond words in order to translate the messages of anger, fear, and hopelessness. Once these messages are heard and understood, healing can begin.

Bridging Worlds was written with the intent of furthering the understanding of the sequelae of child abuse. The presentation of such problems in adolescents often makes it difficult for adults to have empathy for the youths involved. While condoning out-of-control behavior is not appropriate, understanding the context within which the behavior developed may help the process of positive change to occur. This book is intended for use by professionals in the fields of mental health, child protection, juvenile justice, and education, as well as by parents and other invested adults. Policymakers at the agency and legislative levels may also benefit from the perspectives offered. To reframe an adolescent's behavior as a result of a child abuse trauma syndrome, with which many troubled youths are struggling, may enhance understanding and treatment of youths, resulting in positive outcomes. It is hoped that broad thinking across agency boundaries and specialized academic training will result in providing better services for teenagers who have been traumatized by child abuse. A vision focusing on the inextricable link between human rights violations and trauma will provide an unambivalent mission statement for policymakers. Without such a perspective, youths may remain inaccurately identified and horribly mistreated. This may result in well-intentioned adults actually contributing to, rather than alleviating, the difficulties faced by these young people.

In this book, Part I, "A New Vision," provides a look at families, and at issues of diversity. Part II, "Structural Change," is an overview of the major systems involved in raising young people. Theory, social policy, and clinical practice are inextricably linked. As such, social policy provides the context within which young people are treated, and this context is outlined.

Part III, "Healing a Generation," explicates Child Abuse Specific Treatment of Trauma (CASTT), a treatment model for adolescent recovery from traumatic stress, which is formulated for direct clinical application. The development of this model stems from the direct clinical work of the authors. Any model must preserve humanity, not destroy it or place it at risk. Therapeutic work must occur very carefully. Youths deserve to be protected and guided by love. Most parents, with competent, dedicated support, can raise successful, happy children. Professional support of parents needs to be in the form of parent/professional partnerships to empower parents in the task of raising healthy children. However, when parents continually are unable to fulfill these responsibilities and are unwilling to accept help, then the care and guidance of a child will need to be delegated to another caregiver—for the child's sake. The creation of a curative environment is one of the primary dimensions of the CASTT treatment model. An illustration of this environment can be made with the following analogy: If a young person breaks a leg, there is a lengthy recovery period, possibly entailing surgery, hospitalization, a cast, and much validation for suffering. The cast holds the injured leg in place just as CASTT holds a psychologically injured child or adolescent in place.

The Appendix sections of this book provide the following: a CASTT intake form; the creative work of a youth described in this book; suggestions for youth advocacy; a CASTT model for children; and an information sheet that can be copied and handed out. Also, throughout this book: actual clinical examples (with identifying information disguised) are provided; and photographs (by Chris Irwin, a Hampden Academy colleague) and drawings (by Joycee Kennedy) are included, to express what words cannot.

It is hoped that this book will provide a springboard for continued discussions about how to help stop the cycle of violence, outrage, and hurt within which many youths find themselves. This book is not based on empirical data, but rather, on the clinical experiences of the authors. As *Bridging Worlds* unfolds, the connections between youth violence, child abuse, and traumatic stress will be described. Assessing and understanding the importance of cultural diversity, as well as the strengths and liabilities of the social institutions directly involved with adolescents, will be explored. Adult intervention can make a positive difference, even if the young people involved do not always communicate that difference in a clear way. Hopefully, as less and less stigma is attached to hardship, whether it is neglect, or physical or sexual abuse, or whether the hardship befalls a youth or an adult, help will be provided right away.

Reclaim

PART I:
A NEW VISION

Hurdling over a sawhorse, a youth remounts his skateboard, veers a sharp ninety degrees to his left, ascends a curb, races down the sidewalk, drops off another curb, hits the uneven street . . . clickety-clack, and pulls up to meet his friends at the entrance to the shopping mall. Deftly dismounting from his board with a weight shift to the rear edge, the youth takes his position beside a friend on the brick wall and lights a cigarette. "F__ the old man!" he fumes, "That's the last time I'm going home."

Young people tend to reflect the images of adult role models. Therefore, it is not unlikely that abused and neglected youths may create the above images in our society. Joseph Campbell (1988), the late scholar, author, and teacher wrote, "A hero is someone who has given his or her life to something bigger than oneself" (Campbell, 1988, p. 151). "Contemplating heroic lives, lives distinguished by physical or psychological courage, and sometimes both, helps to fortify one's own soul and inspire one to be a little better than deep down, one worries one is" (Epstein, 1991, p. 336).

These youths are heroes, albeit often misguided ones. Their heroism results from their creative survival techniques. The hardships they have endured are frequently beyond the scope of understanding of many professionals. An individual's ability to survive hardships such as physical, sexual, and emotional abuse is heroic in itself. "Children in the United States are five times more likely to be murdered and 12 times more likely to die because of a firearm than those in other industrialized countries" (*Rocky Mountain News*, 1997, February 7, p. 3A). The Centers for Disease Control (CDC) studied twenty-six countries between 1990 and 1995; the CDC reported, "Five countries—Denmark, Ireland, New Zealand, Scotland, and Taiwan—reported no intentional firearm-related deaths among children under 15" (*Rocky Mountain News*, 1997, February 7, p. 3A).

It is the responsibility of all adults to pay attention to the ways in which they have contributed to the harm of children and adolescents. Of equal importance is the need to help youths heal from exposure to such violence.

Society has yet to build an appropriate track channeling the heroism of these youths. Teenagers who have overcome and endured traumatic heritages have developed the power and beauty of the vintage Porsche—with dignity and grace acquired from years of racing.

Current tracks for American teenagers who have experienced severe child abuse include detention centers, departments of special education, hospitals, foster or group homes, and day treatment centers. Unfortunately, parents are sometimes excluded from meetings, and when they are included, they are often blamed for their teenager's difficulties. Family structure is sometimes scapegoated, but in and of itself, it does not cause child abuse. Diversity in cultural heritage is often scapegoated and misunderstood. Cultural diversity plays an important role in identity development throughout childhood. The reality for many of these youths is that they have unique family structures. Not all of the caretakers of these youths are abusive. A new vision of families is important.

Chapter 1

Families

There was a time when the term "family values" generally referred to bargains at a fast-food restaurant. It has now been taken over by politicians to refer to alleged mainstream mores that have supposedly been on the decline in the United States. A lack of family values has been blamed for such diverse issues as alcohol and drug use, sexuality between anyone except married heterosexuals, and gang violence.

This political rhetoric collapses under scrutiny, however. A significant number of traditional families are responsible for a great deal of violence in this country. Physical, sexual, and emotional abuse of children within the context of nuclear families is far from unusual. Such abuse often occurs uninterrupted throughout generations. No socioeconomic, racial, or ethnic group is immune to the victimization of children by family members. While the verbalized value may be that children are not to be treated as objects, the latent message is often in direct contradiction to such a premise.

Nuclear families have been attributed considerable power. In political campaigns, such families are often cited as a source of strength, as well as an endangered structure due to the increase in alternative family forms. The following are some of the factors often cited as contributors to increasing stress for teenagers: the rising divorce rate, the increase of single-parent households, and the increase of two-working-parent households. There are many experts who view these factors as directly contributing to adolescent trauma. In some ways they may be influential in the problems that affect teenagers in these environments. Certainly the divorce process often leaves a single-parent home devoid of the resources needed to keep a parent and children in a close relationship. The government, courts, and legal system are increasing their vigilance to ensure that the absent parent shares resources responsibly. However, many of these families remain economically poor, but are relationally rich.

The nuclear family does not represent everyone's experience, nor is it even considered ideal for many people. The term *family of creation* is used in this work in an effort to include the many creative family configurations to which people belong. The parental composition of the family environment—whether it consists of both biological parents, adoptive parents, stepparents, foster parents, gay or lesbian parents, one parent, or no parents (grandparents often inherit the offspring of their children)—does not have to create traumatic stress. Of importance is not the structure of the family, but the quality of connection within it. Some adults in our society have few positive leadership skills. They may lie and manipulate to get their way, and are often self-centered and self-seeking. These adults will have difficulty providing a rich psychological environment for teenagers. Youths will most likely experience healthy development under the guidance of one or more good adult role models. An adult needs to have his or her own life under control to raise a child well. Such adults must have a developed sense of responsibility, ethical standards, and a strong interest in providing the direction needed to help youths make the transition into the adult world with educated minds and healthy bodies.

Adolescents will painfully attempt to adapt to a variety of living arrangements that represent unhealthy environments. The experiences they suffer during this very vulnerable stage in their lives lay important foundation blocks for adulthood. Too often young people suffer in environments where people are mugged, robbed, or raped regularly. They live with drug and alcohol abuse in their own homes as well as being surrounded by it in the neighborhood. Teenagers suffer from lack of resources needed to make the most of educational opportunities. A self-conscious, hungry adolescent will not take the best advantage of a classroom discussion. In the worst cases, young people suffer parental neglect—even abandonment, and physical, sexual, and verbal abuse. Two unfortunate foundation blocks put in place under these conditions are fear and distrust. These are traits of a soldier at war.

Mass media can also have a deep impact on a child's development. Children and adolescents are exposed regularly to violent images on television, whether real or fictitious. They may hear adults talking about current events. The degree to which a young person's development is affected by hearing about deaths in Somalia, riots in Los Angeles, civil war in Rwanda, the passage of anti-gay legislation in Colorado, and the shooting of a child down the street may vary from individual to individual. Such images, however, do shape young people's beliefs about themselves and the world around them.

In addition, many adult role models have become the subjects of TV news for committing murders, perpetrating fraud, harassing women, embezzling company funds, sexually assaulting young children, being obsessed with careers while neglecting family members, stockpiling vast sums of money while ignoring charity, and demonstrating sexual promiscuity.

One of the remarkable, yet often frustrating qualities of adolescents is their ability to sense reality amid adult mirages, such as the hypocrisy of the parent who asks his or her teenager not to drink, and comes home himself or herself intoxicated from parties most weekends. In other words, teenagers are not easily fooled. One of the developmental tasks of childhood involves internalizing societal values. Many of these values may not be acknowledged as valid by those in power, but the presence of such values is seen in the daily lives of many. Indeed, teenage violence may be a logical, although terrifying, response to adult hypocrisy. An example is Gina Grant, who murdered her brutally abusive mother. Gina, a popular, bright fourteen year old, was taught appropriate behavioral conduct from birth, but experienced her mother's opposite enactments. There was a convoluted logic to the brutal act Gina committed.

THE GANG FAMILY—AN ADOLESCENT RESPONSE

Tracy Chapman (1992) provided a vivid portrayal of adolescent violence, and the lack of adult accountability to such violence, in her song, "Bang Bang Bang." The lyrics explore adults providing weapons to youth, as well as attempting to placate young people without giving them what they truly need. "You go and give the boy a gun/Now there ain't no place to run to."

The children of our society are not only killing adults, they are literally killing each other. News accounts are filled with stories about gang involvement, often termed "senseless violence" by the media. While it may be deplorable, frightening, and upsetting, it is anything but senseless. To many of the adolescents involved, a gang is a family of creation.

While degrees of structure vary from one gang to another, most have clear membership criteria, initiation rituals, and rules by which to live. Certain clothing, peer groups, activities, and language are acceptable. Any behavior outside of a range of activity is suspect or dangerous. Values are generally clear as well. For example, a high degree of loyalty between members exists, and membership is meant to last a lifetime.

The parallels between traditional family groups and gangs are interesting to consider. Families generally have clear norms, expectations, and rules. If someone joins the family, through marriage or birth for example, a range of rituals has been established as rites of passage into the family. Families often have similar cultural and ethnic backgrounds, and socioeconomic status. Membership is meant to last a lifetime, but if someone wishes to leave the family, there are rituals designed for that as well. Gangs and families have the potential to fulfill needs of affiliation, protection, and structure. In a chaotic world, people tend to gravitate toward the familiar. The same is true when resources are scarce, or when real or perceived danger is present.

Shanika's Story

Shanika is a seventeen-year-old African-American young woman who lives in a war zone in the United States. Many of her friends and acquaintances have been injured or killed by other young people. Much of this has been the result of gang violence. Shanika probably turned to gangs for many reasons. Both of her parents are dependent on drugs and/or alcohol. She has been raised primarily by extended family, one of whom has acted as a primary caretaker for Shanika whenever life with her mother became too dangerous. She has not had contact with her father for quite some time. He has been peripherally involved in her life, at best.

Shanika was articulate in discussing her participation in gangs, although she was initially quite guarded about it. In much the same way as a young person might feel protective of her own family,

Shanika relayed information about her gang life carefully. Her ambivalence about gang involvement is similar to her ambivalence about her biological family. Both supply some needs at times, but at incredible emotional and physical costs. The ways in which Shanika had to compromise herself in her families of choice and origin have been life threatening at times.

On one occasion, Shanika was accompanied to court by her mother, grandmother, and therapist. Shanika's mother was clearly inebriated. This was the first time she had come to court to support Shanika in any way. Shanika's conflicted feelings about her mother were clear at this point, as she attempted to justify her mother's actions.

The following is a transcription of an interaction between Shanika and her therapist:

Shanika: My momma's sick again. She has to go to the doctor.
Therapist: Your mom doesn't seem to take very good care of herself.
Shanika: Why do you think I always want to be over there?
Therapist: You take care of her when you're there?
Shanika: Yeah. No one else does.
Therapist: I see. Well, who takes care of you?
Shanika: No one. I do.
Therapist: Doesn't give you much of a chance to just be a kid.
Shanika: Nope.

Examples of adult misunderstanding occurred when Shanika was briefly hospitalized for self-destructive behavior. While she was angry at her therapist at first, the goal of the hospitalization was clearly spelled out for her—Shanika needed to be safe. The therapist hoped for a short hospitalization to stabilize Shanika. A fairly quick return to home and day treatment was sought.

The hospital decided upon different goals for Shanika after working with her for two days. Because she had at one point been involved in gangs, they felt that she needed long-term inpatient psychiatric treatment in order to break her connections with other gang-involved youth. They were willing to certify her to accomplish this goal, which was more possible prior to the impact of managed care. The day-treatment therapist strongly disagreed with this recommendation and was willing to fight for Shanika's return to home and day treatment. It seemed extremely unrealistic and inappropriate to attempt to break Shanika's ties to her family, community, and friends. Her family of creation felt threatened by the staff of the psychiatric hospital. Even though her connections may not have been ideal, attempting to disconnect her seemed cruel and pointless. Helping Shanika survive and grow in the context of her world was the goal of her day treatment.

In addition to the psychiatric staff difficulties, Shanika had a court date for a municipal charge two days after she was hospitalized. When her grandmother called to inform the court that Shanika could not attend due to her hospitalization, she was told by a clerk that a warrant would be issued for her arrest for nonappearance. The clerk would not allow Shanika's grandmother to speak with anyone else about this matter. Her grandmother called the day treatment therapist for assistance with the legal system.

Shanika was not in shape to leave the hospital for any reason at that point. When the therapist called to advocate on Shanika's behalf, she spoke to the person who had previously denied any assistance to the grandmother. After identifying herself as Shanika's therapist to the clerk, it was confirmed that she had told the grandmother that a warrant would be issued if Shanika did not show up. She then very politely connected the therapist to the deputy district attorney in charge of the case. Upon speaking to him and explaining the situation, the attorney not only agreed that Shanika should not come to court, but he actually dropped the charges completely since she was receiving mental health treatment.

The contrast in the treatment, process, and outcome of these phone calls was a fruitful topic of discussion with Shanika, her grandmother, and the therapist. Based on voice alone, a clerk was in the position to decide the outcome of a young woman's nonappearance in court. The grandmother was African American and on public assistance. The therapist was white and employed as a professional. By merely identifying herself as a therapist over the phone, she was able to have the charges completely dropped. Whether this was the result of racism or classism, it was clearly an example of inhumane and disrespectful treatment. This is an example of the institutionalized ambivalence in which young people are caught.

The differences between the worlds of the therapist and Shanika had the potential to thwart connection. Instead, they bridged their worlds by acknowledging their differences and exploring their common ground. This became the basis for the therapeutic relationship.

On one occasion, the therapist was giving Shanika a ride home. Transportation was part of the structure of the day treatment program. At a traffic light, she saw some friends in the next car and started to laugh.

Therapist: What are you laughing about?
Shanika: Never mind (giggling and looking at the other car).
Therapist: Do you know them?
Shanika: Yeah. They just gave me a funny look.
Therapist: How come?
Shanika: Never mind (still giggling).
Therapist: Are they trying to figure out what you're doing in a car with some white woman?
Shanika: Yeah. They'll think I'm trippin'. They've never seen me in a white person's car. Yours is the only one I've been in.
Therapist: Well, I'm honored. What's it like for you to be seen in my car?
Shanika: It's cool, but it just made me think that it's kind of weird.
Therapist: What do you mean?
Shanika: I never thought about it being weird until I saw my friends. I usually don't trust white people, and here we are driving down the street.
Therapist: Is it like we've talked about before, how we try to find the place where our worlds can meet?
Shanika: Yeah, and right now it's in your car!

THE FOSTER FAMILY—
A CREATION OF REMARKABLE LOVE

Many adolescents with child abuse backgrounds are partially raised in foster care. Foster homes represent an important family structure in society.

Tony's Story

Tony's struggle to define his own freedom and his own track was quite creative. He wrote the following poem in 1988:

> Something's screaming within my brain,
> Please don't let me go insane.
> Take my hand and guide me through,
> Introduce me to the truth.
> Remove the darkness so I can see,
> The emotions of reality.
> Show me to the shining light,
> So I can stand and I can fight.

Tony was placed in numerous foster homes during his "foster child career," and he did stand and fight, just as he stated in his poem. It is fair to say that Tony's distrust of humanity was a driving force in his life. In fact, his irreverence toward the adult world made it particularly difficult for his foster parents to be the "guiding light" in his life. But this sixteen-year-old boy believed, in his own mind, that he was disenfranchised by society. Unfortunately, the horrifically violent nature of his biological father had taken a tragic toll, and he felt that he needed to make a statement to the adults who encumbered his world. The following is an edited and storied version of what foster care was like for Tony as an adolescent:

The coarse concrete is behind me. Now I'm strutting along on the smooth and shiny asphalt, no cracks or buckled slabs caused by tree roots. Around a circle of expensive Colonial and Tudor mansions I traverse, a cigarette hanging from my mouth and my freshly shaven head gleaming in the sun. When the weather is warm like this, I like to wear my Grateful Dead T-shirt. But when it cools down, I'll wear my flight jacket, almost always with jeans but sometimes with fatigues. I feel meaner and more subversive when I wear fatigues. Occasionally, I will wear Bugle Boys but rarely will I wear shorts. I hate shorts because my legs are somewhat scrawny and "prison pallor" white. Basically, my clothes define who I am or at least who I feel I am, a Skinhead. The Dr. Martens on my feet prove it.

Having lived in a large, nice house this past year, it's not been easy to maintain the image I have of myself. It has been comfortable and safe but it's not me. Hell, I can't find me anyway—no matter how hard I try. Several nights ago, when my foster family was out, I trundled on over to "Possum's" on my bike. His apartment was over by the University of Denver in a basement of a house about five blocks from the campus. The "cordial" welcome message on the old wooden outer door was painted in black. "F— you Laskin," it said. It was a perverse form of welcome that made you feel like an insider. Four of my friends were hanging out on the floor, toking from a joint of "killer dope." Possum was slung in a tattered chair drinking vodka. I settled into a rumpled sleeping bag on the floor, kind of in the middle of things. Ashtrays were crowded on one small, cracked, and stained wood-and-formica table. The walls were etched and painted with graffiti of the foulest kind. As I poured a drink, Possum led the Skinhead creed:

"We the people of the Federation of United Skinheads, under the oath to extend loyalty and compassion for our own, are one nation under God, with liberty and justice for us. We live to maim! We live to kill! We live to hate! More power to us! More power to us!"

Feeling totally exhilarated after that, I proceeded to get high. My friends each debriefed me about my experience of living with the filthy rich, as they perceived my home life. Their main advice was . . . "Take everything you can."

Jason started passing around sheets given to him the night before at a big meeting of Skinheads. An L.A. Skin had arrived in town to do some training. Possum read aloud the handout, titled "The National Nazi Rebellion":

1. To show racism,
2. To protect the white race at any cost,
3. To love any member of the National Nazi Rebellion (N.N.R.),
4. To accept the authority of members in a higher position,
5. To fight violence with violence, and
6. To stand together as the united force of fear.

I felt good. All my emotions were left behind. I was a flesh-and-blood machine feeding on dogma. I was in my own world, my own realm—living with and for myself with my own kind.

It was not the same in my foster home. One of my foster parents was Jewish! Not only that, my foster parents had all the awful beliefs that Jews and others have, like do well in your studies. They enrolled me in this tough inner-city high school, a product of busing legislation, to be another token upper-class white. I saw through this clouded motivation and ditched my classes . . . not that I wanted to attend anyway. My foster brother and sister could mingle with the blacks and play equal while I played the reality of the situation; I did not belong to this social set. And I wouldn't go. My friends would not go either.

The already precarious foster-home placement was jeopardized by my frequent all-night absences, during which I bunked out at Possum's. There was this one "chick" who was a wannabe Skin with whom I would get it on occasionally. It was never clear in my mind whether it was the Jewish temple or my foster mother who disapproved of premarital sex. I didn't really care. The shock and disbelief often expressed by my foster mother was sometimes disconcerting, particularly when she saw the swastikas in the margins of my school papers . . . the products of my daydreaming and doodling. I was just not in a position to handle my life in any socially acceptable fashion.

As the school year progressed, so did the parade of friends into my closet and behind my bed. Knowing that the 'rents [short for parents] wouldn't let friends stay overnight during the school week, I let them into the house late at night, after everyone went to bed. They would hide in my closet or between my bed and the wall if they heard someone coming downstairs. Rick moved in for three days and no one else in the house knew. In the morning, Rachel, my foster sister, drove me to school. That was her responsibility, assigned by her mother. After walking into the school building for a few minutes, for effect only, I doubled back to the house on my skateboard to meet Rick. By this time both parents had left for work—an advantage that goes with two parents working outside the home. We just needed to make sure we cleaned up and didn't set the house on fire in the process.

On the days I ditched school, I usually didn't do much. As a matter of fact my whole life was . . . not doing much. It was one of the few things I did well. Anyway, when I got back to the house I fixed omelettes, carefully cleaning up afterward to cover my tracks. Rick sometimes left after breakfast. Sometimes, he stayed longer. I don't even know where he went. Kids like Rick and I were basically nomads. We had no goals.

At night, I hung out on the back patio, watching the clouds move across the sky. The tarnished ashtray, on a makeshift patio table fashioned from a large public utility wire spool, was heaped with months of charred cigarette butts. The table was surrounded by four chairs. Mine was the one facing southwest. This was my place. My foster parents didn't often join me when I was smoking my cigarettes. They couldn't handle the secondary smoke and the ashtray labeled "disgusting" that I generally refused to empty.

Also, on the patio, I was safe from my beautiful blond sister. She was a senior at my high school, an honor student, editor of the yearbook, and other such crap. Eric, my foster brother, never bothered me much. He was a sophomore, a great basketball player, also with good grades. Eric had blond curly hair. He wasn't bad looking.

My foster father tried from time to time to get to know me. He took me shopping, shot baskets with me, encouraged me to try in school. He wasn't a bad dude, but I considered him to be a graying fool. My foster mother loved me. She would sometimes cry when I was around. Despite her loyalty to me, she seemed to feel guilty about my influence on her kids.

I used to feel peaceful sitting on the patio. On the patio I wasn't angry with anyone. As a young child I had once even tried to strangle another kid in front of social studies class. A teacher had to intervene. I could have hurt anyone and anything in those days. When I was around eleven and on the run, a cat kept following me. I was numb and I didn't care about the cat dead or alive. I knifed it.

The good thing about this foster home was that I had my own kitten, an ironic commentary, considering the cat-knifing episode. In fact I asked my foster mother if I could bring the kitten with me when I came to live with her. My foster mother agreed, thinking that my having a pet could be an integral part of my rehabilitation. She did not know that I had killed a pet at a previous time in my life. Strangely, I gave the kitten loads of attention, perhaps to atone for my earlier grievous act. My foster mother would always say, "Your kitten is the sweetest animal we have ever had living in the house." The neighborhood children loved my pet, too. I named the kitten "Reefer" because she liked to eat grass. Of course, my foster mother recognized that reefer is slang for a marijuana cigarette. She refused to let me call her that, so I agreed to call her "Becky"—after a girl I had liked.

I saw a psychologist weekly on Tuesday afternoons at two o'clock. My foster father left work early on those days to take me to the doctor's office. The shrink was a pretty nice dude who had reams of history about my past. It never helped. He still knew squat about me. I never told him about the cat. Often when I sat out on the patio I would go over some of our sessions in my mind.

"How did your week go, Tony?"

"OK. Did you get your hair cut, Dr. Lewis?"

"This session is for you, Tony."

"My life is boring. I go to school, I come home and sit on the patio. I watch TV, I go to bed, and get up and go to school again. What's there to talk about?"

"Can you tell me something about school?"

"I hate school! My teachers suck and I want them to die."

I had a great time on the patio, sometimes sitting for hours reminiscing about the hours of therapeutic bullshit. Unfortunately, since I was a bullshit artist in my own right, my situation did not improve. Every weekend I was at Possum's drinking and doing drugs. Mondays started to be a problem because I could not get up. Then I stopped coming home on Sunday nights. Finally, Dr. Lewis committed me to the hospital—rightfully so, because if anyone was on the verge of losing it, it was me.

It wasn't as if I had never been in the hospital before, but I had a long way back this time, mainly just getting off the alcohol and drugs. My foster mother visited me weekly; my foster father and the foster sibs came at least every other week. I was kept in lock-up about two months. I was jumpy on the unit and remained afraid to address the traumatic experiences of my life, such as watching my natural dad trying to slit my mother's throat.

During visits, I freaked out my foster mother with my bizarre behavior. I remember one night dancing from the radiator to the bed, back to the radiator. I just didn't care how crazy I acted. Whatever felt good at the time, I did. This hospitalization, like the others, did not help.

It was a crisp winter morning when I put my foster family to the extreme test of tolerance. Rick had spent the night on the floor behind my bed in an old sleeping bag. I was up and ready to go to school with Rachel. I was looking particularly well, sporting my new Topsiders, my Grateful Dead T-shirt, and a CB jacket. I even had a bit of hair that had grown out in the hospital. I entered school through the south entrance of school, walked down the hall, and out the north entrance. It was about nine o'clock in the morning when I slithered through the back door at home, having circled back for the umpteenth time since my stay at this foster home. I called Dan to come over and the three of us gathered in the kitchen for omelettes. I chopped up small morsels of cheese, onions, peppers, and bacon. As we enjoyed our breakfast, we made plans to remove the old decals from our skateboards. Dan had brought over red and black paint and paint brushes to repaint the boards. Rick was to sketch original drawings on the boards before we painted.

Dan was an OK dude—at least I thought he was. He was a couple of inches taller than I—probably six feet, with bright red hair. I had dull red hair. He was normal looking but had an over-abundance of freckles. He wore Dr. Martens and a flight jacket. It was standard wear for any self-respecting Skin. Dan, however, was not an official Skinhead. Rick was a pure Skin. Anyway, Rick had been on the run on and off for the last year. He hadn't seen his mother in months and pretended he didn't give a shit. His dad was the problem. Whenever Rick brought home school grades that were substandard, he would get it with a belt. His dad had been in therapy and Rick had been in therapy, but still Rick brought home rotten grades and would get his punishment through the painful end of a leather belt. Rick solved the problem for himself by not going home anymore, nor did he go to school. His situation made me nervous because the cops were always looking for him.

After we scraped and scoured the dishes I went to the garage to get the Coleman lantern fluid. The best approach, I thought, was to light the decals on fire to let them burn off. Then the plan was, using sandpaper from my foster father's workbench, to sand the boards in preparation for Rick to etch his drawings on the boards. After that, we intended to paint them. We arranged the brushes, paint, lantern fluid, rags, matches, sandpaper, and cigarettes carefully on the kitchen table. No drugs of any sort would be used that day. We had work to do.

I started by pouring lantern fluid on the top of my board and set it ablaze. The flames danced as the shellac and decals dripped to the floor. When the flames died down, I blew them out. I cradled my singed board in my arms and started to sand. The board gradually took on a smooth, shiny appearance. This was fun. It sure beat learning about verb tenses and pronoun references.

It was Dan's turn. He poured the lantern fluid on his board, lit it and sent it flaming across the long span of kitchen floor. He wanted to light all three boards on fire and build a flaming armada. My board was looking too good to engage in such folly.

Rick went next and this is when everything began to get f— up. As he poured the fluid onto his board, he poured a large amount on his blue denim shirt. When he put the match to his skateboard, his shirt went up in flames, too.

There Rick was, engulfed in flames, and Dan and I were in a panic. Dan was of no help. He yelled, "Christ we have to get out of here!" and "Wow! Jesus! What should we do?" He then ran to his car and sped off God only knows where. I was numb. I stared at my best friend going up in flames. Rick was screaming. I thought to myself I should get out of the house too or I would be dead meat.

Instead, I grabbed a blanket, wrapped it around Rick, and in a bear hug threw him to the floor and rolled around on the kitchen floor with him until the flames went out. Then I took him up to the shower and doused him in cold water. At this point, I thought he would be OK. My next thought was to clean up the kitchen and get the hell out of the house. No such luck. Rick was in great pain, crying wildly, "Tony, I can't stand the pain!" As the shadows of my past irresponsibility began to surface and haunt me, I picked up the phone and called 911. I amazed myself. I had changed. I exhibited some sense and responsibility in handling a dire situation. Rick was taken to a hospital and was treated on a special burn unit for two weeks. I visited him daily. He lived and I was proud that I was instrumental in saving his life.

All adults are Tony's parents. Adults created the atmosphere in which this young man struggles. The life of many American teenagers, in their own eyes, is overwhelming. It is imperative for society to provide families for Tony's healing.

When the behavior of a youth becomes erratic and incorrigible at home, or the youth is in danger from physical, sexual, or emotional abuse, he or she may be placed in foster care. It happens in families where the teenager repeatedly commits crimes, lives in unhealthy conditions, is truant or abandoned, or in any other of a number of situations where the current home situation is found not to be in the best interest of the young person.

During the time an adolescent is placed in foster care, the inner turmoil of the youth usually mixes with a foreign environment which places intense early pressure on the foster parents. They are required to "dance fast" in order to stay in step with the new situation. Foster care is a system that supports a kind of "in-country" exile for these teenagers. These youths are like foreigners, but in their own country. They are often out of step with their own culture. Tony's story provides an inside lens for the reader to view a young boy identifying with white supremacy. This boy's social development, moral development, and educational development had been derailed by child abuse. Foster parents need to learn the culture of trauma.

As a family makes a decision to become foster parents of an adolescent, the family must realize that they will be accepting into their home a youth who, more often than not, will be troubled by a disrupted, chaotic, difficult past. The youth will not likely be a shy but courteous teenager who will answer questions politely. More likely the youth will respond with silence, sullenness, or hostility.

Behavioral Masking of Trauma

The range of behavior that is considered healthy in adolescence is vast. Healthy youths experiment with many behavioral styles before settling on one that is comfortable for them and at the same time socially acceptable. Adolescents in foster care display a much different type of behavior because most suffer the effects of trauma.

The following story describes the early childhood of another teenager in foster care:

Alex's Story

As a small girl, Alex played in the Colorado woods. The summer sun kept her warm among the shadows—until she was locked in her room for eight hours by her adoptive parents. Then, Alex was six years old.

Alex was born in a tenement house somewhere in Colorado. Just before the age of two she was retrieved by a local sheriff together with her two siblings, one six months, the other about three years old. The children had been unattended for days. They were starving and their living conditions were filthy. Alex was found with cigarette burns covering her body and a dent in the back of her skull. During the trial where her mother, a prostitute, was tried for child abuse, the judge had tears in his eyes. Alex's father was already in prison on other charges.

Shortly after the trial, Alex was adopted by the Franklins, who had no children of their own. Not long after Alex moved into the Franklins' house, Mrs. Franklin became pregnant with the first of her three biological children. It was at this time Alex first felt rejected by her adoptive parents.

The relationship between Alex and her adoptive parents could easily be characterized as traumatic. The Franklins complained of Alex's chronic ear infections and a hospitalization for pneumonia. When Alex was ill, the Franklins felt that she was stubborn and defiant. Alex would panic and throw hysterical tantrums.

Alex felt neither loved nor understood by her adoptive parents. The Franklins, embarrassed to take her anywhere, kept her isolated at home. In an effort to control Alex's tantrums, the Franklins locked her in her room and rigged an alarm to alert them if she tried to escape. In the months and years after Alex's adoption, she was seen by approximately fifteen professionals—psychiatrists, psychologists, and social workers—before she was admitted to a private psychiatric hospital. She was hospitalized by her psychiatrist after complaining about hearing voices and for displaying violent episodes of screaming and tearing her hair out. It was during this time that Alex admitted she tried to commit suicide. According to Alex, the doctors administered electroshock therapy. It is possible that Alex may have misconstrued brain scans given in the hospital as electric shock treatments. The Franklins were convinced that Alex's behavior was bizarre and even psychotic. The hospital's report indicated paranoia.

It is unclear how long Alex was at this small hospital before being moved to a state hospital. Alex was at the state hospital about a year and then transferred to a group home. Alex described the group home as having a rigid behavior management system. In spite of the structure, the youths frequently stole each others' possessions. Alex hated the home and she successfully sabotaged her stay there—primarily by running away, only to be readmitted to the state hospital.

The running continued even after her return to the state hospital. During one incident, when a security officer tried to apprehend her, she attacked him with a meat fork. Her caseworker felt she should be discharged from the state hospital but was conflicted about where to place her. The agency refused to consider the adoptive parents for placement because they showed little interest in Alex during her hospitalization. They visited irregularly, refused to participate in therapy, and repeatedly forgot to acknowledge her birthday. But the caseworker was convinced that Alex needed parenting badly, and subsequently placed her in a foster home. This was about five years later. Alex was entering adolescence.

The behavior of adolescents in foster care is not forthright. It is often false, almost preposterous. These young people, too, experiment with different behavioral styles, but much of it does not reflect their true feelings. Instead they present the opposite in behavior. Anna Freud (1966) captured the zest and unpredictability of the general stage of adolescence:

> In nonanalytic writings we find many striking descriptions of the changes which take place in character during these years, of the disturbances in the psychic equilibrium, and above all, of the incomprehensible and irreconcilable contradictions then apparent in the psychic life. Adolescents are excessively egoistic, regarding themselves as the center of the universe and the sole object of interest, and yet at no time in later life are they capable of so much self-sacrifice and devotion. They form the most passionate love relations, only to break them off as abruptly as they began them. On one hand, they throw themselves enthusiastically into the life of the community and, on the other, they have an overpowering longing for solitude. They oscillate between blind submission to some self-chosen leader and defiant rebellion against any and every authority. They are selfish and materially minded and at the same time

full of lofty idealism. They are ascetic but will suddenly plunge into instinctual indulgence of the most primitive character. At times their behavior to other people is rough and inconsiderate yet they themselves are extremely touchy. Their moods veer between light-hearted optimism and the blackest pessimism. Sometimes they will work with indefatigable enthusiasm and at other times they are sluggish and apathetic. (pp. 137-138)

It is the traumatized adolescent, lacking in self-confidence to struggle with the inconsistencies described by Anna Freud, who flounders in accomplishing the lessons of growth. The unhelped traumatized adolescent hides his or her insecurity behind a mask. The tragedy here is that often, troubled adolescents become trapped behind these masks. Figuratively, traumatized adolescents, without appropriate help, are capable of living lives of continual masks. They develop phony, meaningless, empty relationships, afraid to reveal more than a facade to others (an example of the potential consequences of the early adaptive response of separation from adults). It is important for foster parents, caseworkers, and therapists to understand this.

Behavioral Responses of Traumatized Youths

The following examples show the means through which adolescents in foster care will try to deceive those around them when they have been traumatized and have failed to recover:

Jo's Story

An attractive, yet insecure fifteen-year-old foster daughter, Jo, asked a popular student to a dance. The boy accepted. After five hours of preparation, she waited worriedly for her date to arrive. He never showed. Devastated by this experience and unable to integrate the disappointment into her psyche, Jo started trying to gain attention from boys by being seductive and engaging in sexual relationships she did not want. At school she portrayed herself as a fast, streetwise girl when in reality she was frightened and insecure. She was, in fact, disgusted by her own behavior.

Sam's Story

This foster daughter received mostly Fs one semester. She attended school, but was unable to concentrate and follow through to the point of completing her assignments. "School sucks!" was her almost-constant rejoinder. After challenging her opinion, Sam's foster parents learned that she did not try in school because she was sure she would fail. Her belief system created a cycle of inertia. Later, she learned that success was preceded by learning how to fail. Three years after this lesson was internalized, Sam was awarded a four-year college scholarship.

Sean's Story

A good-looking, long-haired, rugged, young foster son, Sean continually intimidated the teachers and students at his school. After several meetings with him, his foster mother learned that his antagonistic attitude was a means to isolate himself from closeness to those around him. The tragedy was that he felt empty inside. His isolation protected his fears of intimacy. His behavior was a facade. Luckily, Sean's foster mother was able to parent him for three years, dissolving the facade with her consistent love and protection.

Anger is the other dynamic that youths traumatized by severe child abuse often display in day-to-day living. In the CASTT model, anger is identified as a variation of hyperarousal. *The American Heritage Dictionary of the English Language* (1981) defines anger as, "A feeling of extreme displeasure, hostility, indignation or exasperation toward someone or something; rage; wrath; ire" (p. 50). The manifestation of anger is degrading and controlling; in its most aggressive form, anger is life-threatening.

Children growing up are often subjected to these manifestations. A teacher can embarrass students by listing math scores in order of achievement on the blackboard. Often a teacher using this strategy is angry at those students who do not properly prepare for a test or may have incurred too many absences. When anger from an adult is expressed in a demeaning manner, it fosters insecurity, anxiety, and low self-esteem in a child or adolescent.

In family relationships, anger is often used to control another family member. An example would be a mother, ignoring the presence of her daughter's friend, screaming, "Why can't you remember to take out the trash?" Anger can produce results, but the use of it is often insensitive. The dignity of the daughter is not maintained when the mother screams at her in front of her friend.

There are many prototypes of potentially life-threatening anger. Some examples might be parents beating their children with belts under the pretext of disciplining, or locking them in a closet until they learn to respect their parents, an ironic twist. Self-anger can be life threatening, manifesting as suicide. In this case, death represents the ultimate form of control.

Teenagers who have been locked in closets for several days, who have been humiliated by caretakers, who have been abandoned at birth, or who have looked to poor role models have learned to express their anger by manipulating, fighting, screaming, cursing, or intimidating others—thus controlling and threatening the lives of others.

Foster parents should be encouraged to teach teenagers to accept angry feelings, together with loving feelings, frustrating feelings, and sad feelings. Foster parents might also consider teaching humility because teenagers will not change the world with their feelings. Their anger does not endow them with omnipotence. Moreover, just as teenagers object to being the target of the wrath of others, they need to learn not to behave in a similar fashion.

A successful foster parent for adolescents needs to dance a fast dance to keep a step ahead of the deceit and anger of a traumatized youth—and also must play a vital role in helping the youth recover. Successful foster parents do not try to control the behavior of these adolescents. Instead, they focus on helping a youth learn to control his or her own behavior by setting collaborated limits and modeling acceptable behavior. Studies often focus on measuring foster care success in terms of the ability to control a youth. Simon and Simon (1982), in their evaluation of the influence of the foster parent training program of Nova University, cited the inability of foster parents to control the child as the primary cause for placement failure. Successful foster parents often give unconditional love to teenagers who manifest out-of-control behavior. This ability is critical because foster family relationships begin in life's midstream without history.

Foster parenting roles differ depending upon the resources and motivation of biological parents. Foster parents must be flexible, compassionate, and understanding. A youth may be in transition to return to biological parents. Foster parents in this circumstance may successfully take on the role of co-parents, helping to rebuild the biological family alliance and recognizing that the youth has membership in two homes.

Wise foster parents do not use derogatory statements concerning biological parents because they know such statements may damage the ego of the youth. An example of a harmful statement would be, "Your mother was no good." A helpful statement would be, "When your mother acted like that, I bet you felt disappointed." When there is not a biological parent available to the youth, then a foster parent must assume the role of primary parent. This role is arduous. If the youth is an adolescent, the natural developmental task is separating and moving toward independence.

As a surrogate parent, a foster parent must have wisdom, maturity and self-discipline. He or she must consistently model high values through the honest sharing of himself or herself, fostering a household atmosphere for growth. Highlighting the beliefs of Otto Fenichel, a respected psychoanalyst and author, Kiell (1964) said, "A person's self-esteem, as well as the content and extent of his defenses depends upon his ideals, which are developed less by direct teaching than by the general spirit that surrounds the growing child" (p. 531).

Endearing foster parents develop loving, supporting relationships with their foster children that continue throughout life. One example is a thirty-five-year-old foster daughter who sang and played the guitar at an important family celebration. This young woman is a loved and respected member of her foster family; their door is always open to her for reaffirmation as she confronts the stages and challenges of her life.

THE ADOPTIVE FAMILY— A SPECIAL, OFTEN FRAGILE FAMILY OF CREATION

Adoption can take place at any time during a child's life. A young person may go through the adoptive and foster care systems, or may be adopted as a newborn infant. Adoptions may be relinquished or lifelong. Many adoptive parents work hard to provide a family for their children, just as many adoptees adapt quite well to their family situations.

Unfortunately, this is not always the case. While adoptees comprise an estimated 2 percent to 3 percent of the population, they tend to be overrepresented in mental health treatment settings (Partridge, 1991). Adoption may become a critical issue during adolescence because of the move toward identity consolidation (LeVine and Sallee, 1990). When complexities such as abuse, placement difficulties, or biologically determined problems have been present in the adopted youth's life, these issues may be exacerbated further. "Under the most ideal circumstances, the adopted child will experience personal stresses as he or she moves toward integration of the adoptive status" (Levine and Sallee, 1990, p. 218).

Adoptees face specific challenges which may become a focus for treatment. One such challenge involves unacknowledged losses, starting with the loss of birth parents (Bertocci and Schechter, 1991; Partridge, 1991). This initial loss is the paradigm upon which other losses revolve, which can result in a loss-related depression for some adoptees. Many adoptees describe a vacuum within themselves which enhances a sense of vulnerability around subsequent losses experienced throughout life (Bertocci and Schechter, 1991). This very basic issue is often overlooked by families and clinicians, perhaps because of the alleged replacement of birth parents with adoptive parents. It is often difficult for adoptive parents to allow the young person to mourn the loss of birth parents (Partridge, 1991). This is true in part because, unlike the death of a loved one, the loss of a birth parent is potentially reversible via a search process. Along with this is an inherent loss of information regarding one's own history, often including basic information about birth parents. This may leave an adoptee attempting to mourn vague concepts instead of real people. Without the context of biological relatedness, adoptees may experience a lack of groundedness in reality, or a sense of being unreal (Partridge, 1991).

Stigmas of Adoption

The word "illegitimate" used to be stamped on the birth certificates of adoptees in some states. This stigmatized adoptees in specific ways, such as inhibiting their ability to be hired for certain jobs requiring a high degree of "morality." While this is no longer the case, the stigma of adoption still exists, albeit on a much more subtle level.

The following story presents numerous complications in terms of adolescent development. The young woman's status as an adoptee is certainly one of the key issues.

Michelle's Story

Michelle was the second child to be adopted into an upper-middle-class family of European descent. Secrecy became a pre-dominant theme in this family. Such secrecy included not only adoption, but severe physical abuse by her older brother, sexual abuse by extended family members, and the alcoholism of various adults. The messages she received concerning adoption invoked shame and a strong sense of abandonment. Such feelings were largely invisible to others in her life, particularly her parents. They were not able to see her accurately, nor were they able to protect her from the violence of others. From outward appearances, this family looked like a highly functioning, socioeconomically privileged unit. Similar to a Hollywood movie set, the outside appearances covered up an emptiness and lack of substance on the part of the family. Michelle played along with her role in the family until she was raped by a member of her family at age eleven. It was at that time that she made her first suicide attempt by stepping in front of a speeding truck on a busy suburban street. The truck avoided hitting her, but the overwhelming sense of loss and loneliness continued.

Because of Michelle's strong academic skills and positive relationships with teachers, she was not perceived as a child with difficulties. She utilized relationships with positive adults in her life to maintain a sense of self-worth. What she did not get at home she sought elsewhere, and what continued at home she tried to mitigate through friendships with peers and adults. School was her sanctuary, the place where she could thrive academically and relationally. Schoolwork was an area within which she had control.

As an adolescent, Michelle became more visibly distant and angry in relation to the only family she had ever known. To further compound her sense of self-loathing, she began to be aware of sexual attraction to members of her own gender. While the initial awareness of one's gay, lesbian, or bisexual identity is complicated in a homophobic culture such as the United States, the addition of this issue to her current life was overwhelming. The self-destructive behavior continued in forms such as mixing various prescription and illegal drugs with alcohol, a kind of pharmaceutical Russian roulette. She also drove recklessly on dangerous roads, sometimes under the influence of some substance. She believed the only way to stop the overwhelming pain in her life was to die.

It is not entirely clear how Michelle managed to survive her childhood reasonably intact. It was not until she entered college and sought out help for herself that she began to allow healing from the various forms of abuse and neglect she had experienced. She eventually searched for, and found, her birth parents, neither of whom wished to have ongoing contact with her. For Michelle, this was a healing experience nonetheless, as she could now mourn the loss of actual people. As an adult, she is comfortable as a lesbian, and is building a family of her own.

The American culture emphasizes the importance of blood ties and physical similarities. Except in cases of open adoption, adoptees may regularly face the fact that they are not allowed access to their own genealogical background. A physician asking for a medical history is one such example. This may result in feelings of envy and loss revolving around basic advantages about which nonadoptees do not have to think. A search for birth parents may serve as an attempt to achieve a greater homeostatic balance (Bertocci and Schechter, 1991) by alleviating the sense of missing out on something very basic.

Tension and secrecy are also key issues for many adoptees (Partridge, 1991). This is likely reflective of the more subtle ways in which adoption is still stigmatized to some degree. "The missing reality is one hurdle, the added atmosphere of tension and secrecy surrounding the reality intensifies the challenge to the adoptee" (Partridge, 1991, p. 201). Secrecy implies a need to hide something shameful. Given that secrets in adoption involve the actual history and circumstances of a person's birth, an assumption may be made by the adoptee that he or she is a bad person. This may be true even if the adoptive family is open, as tension could exist in the extended family or larger society. For adolescents in particular, adoptees may constantly test their families by acting out to see if they are still lovable under difficult circumstances. Other adolescents may feel compelled to be unusually good to prevent being sent away (Partridge, 1991).

Issues regarding invisibility and mirroring may also be present for adoptees. The importance of being accurately seen and understood by significant others is essential from a self-in-relation perspective. "Another path to disempowerment and the paralyzing experience of shame, is to be treated as if one is invisible and inaudible" (Jordan, 1989, p. 7). A sense of connectedness is affirmed in this culture via stories about physical similarities. This does not happen for adopted children, as there may be silence instead. Adoptees are also lacking visual cues regarding physical similarities (Partridge, 1991). In Michelle's case, she did not look like her adoptive parents, while her brother did. As an adolescent, these differences became even more apparent and were derogatorily commented upon by her mother. In transracial adoptions, this may be a more obvious issue as well. Children adopted into families from a different ethnic background are constantly reminded that they are different just by their physical appearance.

Making connections with others is a related area of difficulty. Fears of abandonment may inhibit adoptees in making relationships with others. For adoptees in therapy, it is important to point out the tenuous connections made by the adoptee, as well as the use of detachment as a means of coping with a threatened loss. Given the need for a sense of connectedness across generations, a desire to search for biological family may be a way of coping with this "psychological amputation" (Bertocci and Schechter, 1991).

A lack of mirroring and sense of invisibility may also have an impact on an adoptee's body image and sexuality. The adopted adolescent's body is a link to the birth parents. This intensifies the meaning of one's physiological being. On some level, adoptees may feel that biological children would have been preferable to adoptive parents, and that adoption was a second choice (Partridge, 1991). In reality, this is often the case. Sexuality may be viewed as hazardous, whether one identifies with the birth parent (fertile) or the adoptive parent (infertile). Sexuality therefore can be associated with loss and punishment, as well as rivalry. As a child develops into more of a sexual being in adolescence, conflict may arise between adoptive parents and their children due to unconscious resentment and jealousy. All of these issues make it important to ask adoptees in treatment about fears and thoughts regarding sexuality, including thoughts about both sets of parents (Bertocci and Schechter, 1991). Apart from sexuality and body image, adoptees may feel a sense of divided identity, as an adoptee is a child both of birth parents and of adoptive parents. Using an analogy of someone who has a bicultural identity may be helpful for some adoptees (Partridge, 1991).

Adoptees experience a sense of differentness from nonadopted peers, and indeed, they are different in some key ways. In a study by Reynolds, Levy, and Eisnitz (1977; cited in Partridge, 1991), adoptees showed a higher anxiety level than prisoners of war. This may reflect the impact of what was likely a stressful and anxious pregnancy on the fetus when a mother is in the process of relinquishing her child. Adoptees may not feel an internal locus of control, as their lives have clearly been shaped by external forces. Searching for one's family of origin may assist an adoptee in shifting the perception of oneself as an agent of change. This clearly challenges the sense of indebtedness to adopted families and the general passivity that adoptees may feel. It is therapeutically important to assist these young people in internalizing a sense of control over their lives (Bertocci and Schechter, 1991) in a safe and healthy way.

Clinicians need to be aware of issues of adoption in working with young people, as struggles with identity issues are key within that developmental stage. Postadoption counseling for adoptive parents may alleviate future difficulties by sensitizing parents to the unique needs of an adopted child. This includes a focus on the importance of honesty and openness regarding questions of origin, as well as a focus on at least the psychological presence of birth parents in the life of an adopted child (Kirschner and Nagel, 1988).

THE BIRTH FAMILY

The commitment that many parents make to their teenagers who have been traumatized by child abuse is profound and courageous. Parents may knowingly not have protected their child from harm, may not have been able to protect their child from harm, or may have actually inflicted harm themselves, disrupting the sacred parent-child bond. The ethical issues in such cases are extremely complex. Because of the tragedy of child abuse and its impact on young people, some parents who make one or two serious mistakes, yet are capable of change with help and guidance, are often unjustly excluded. It is important to make careful assessments of parental strengths because parents who have suffered trauma themselves can benefit from understanding and guidance. Some parents can be helped to recover and then these same parents can become bastions of strength, able to reach out and help their children heal.

Sometimes parents are on the edge of being able to provide safe, healthy environments for their children. Some days these parents seem calm and capable of empathy and other days they enter into either an emotional, cognitive, or physical state of being unable to care for a young person. Why this parental inconsistency may occur is a complicated question. In today's world, the detractors from effective parenting are many. Some parents lack resources and support systems. Ecological factors, such as poor educational resources, neighborhood violence, and inadequate health care cause family hardship. Career fulfillment demands of parents often compete with the needs of young people. Mothers and fathers who wish to be successful at their jobs are pulled away from spending time at home. When a parent responds to the pull from home, she or he may lose the job. Layoffs from work are common in American society today. The impact of these kinds of stresses on young people can be dramatic. An illustration would be the father who is laid off from work and is emotionally tormented and exhausted when he comes home. His ten-year-old son shoots him with his new high-powered squirt gun. The father hits his son with a two-by-four.

Many parents do not have the support of extended family to help guide their teenagers through milestones, such as biological changes in puberty. Milestones often become stressors rather than normal challenges of adolescence. Often parents who are under significant stress miss the point of what is going on with their teenagers. An example of misunderstanding in parenting might be characterized by the fifteen-year-old daughter who tells her mother about her boyfriend going out "on the sly" with another girl. The mother's dissonant response to helping her daughter is to tell her, "Grow up!" (assuming the daughter understands and accepts that in some relationships partners are unfaithful). The mother is unable to empathically connect with her daughter.

Another illustration of cognitive dissonance between a parent and a child is represented by the following list that a parent made for his fourteen-year-old son:

Peter's Rules

Break these rules and you no longer can live at home (no explanation is given to the fourteen-year-old about where he might go to live):

1. Do not get suspended or expelled, or leave school without permission.
2. Come straight home after school.
3. Do not go anywhere without prior permission.
4. Do not have contact with Sam and Susan until you are eighteen years old.
5. Do not go into the yard without prior permission.
6. Do not lie.

Illness can interfere with good parenting. Illness of an at-home parent can create an emotional separation of a youth from a parent when a parent lacks the energy to give quality time to a youth. Illness that requires a parent to be hospitalized can preclude a parent-child connection unless there are supportive services encouraging a youth to visit a hospitalized parent.

Legal action can physically separate a youth from his or her parent. Parents who are jailed will not be able to assume the role of parent. Parents who have been separated from their children because of child abuse allegations may only be able to assume a parenting role with close supervision.

The final group of parents cannot or will not raise their children in a healthy atmosphere. These are parents who suffer from extreme mental illness, moral depravity, or both. Examples of parents who would fall into this category are Jennifer Reali and Joseph Steinberg. Jennifer Reali was convicted of murdering her lover's wife in Colorado. In New York, Joseph Steinberg was convicted of murdering his child. Other adults will need to help each Reali child create a corrected life story. The Steinberg child was robbed of that chance.

Perhaps most parents have strengths that they are unaware of. What may look like inappropriate parenting on the outside is often providing vital lifelines to children. Therefore, to therapists who specialize in stopping child abuse, the challenges of helping parents resolve the ambivalences of vice and virtue, of suffering and forgiveness, of victimization and social responsibility, must be met. These strengths, challenges, and resolutions are illustrated by the following story:

A Father's Story

An alcoholic father beat his son regularly with a leather strap from ages five to ten. The boy was removed from the home several times by a child protection agency. Finally, the father entered a residential alcohol program and to this date has experienced many years of sobriety. The parents, determined to hang on, struggled gallantly with the aid of professionals to help the boy struggle through adolescence. The mother, father, one sister, and the boy believed that the psychological trauma from the previously unsafe environment could be overcome. Once the father had gained consistent sobriety, he shifted his focus to collaborate with professionals and his wife to reorganize his home, now providing for the physical and emotional safety of his children. This father had tremendous courage and strength of character. He took the lead in bringing his family back to health from a point of a shattered existence. He was able to master corrected behavior, such as hugging his son, letting his son know that the boy had always been valuable and special, and admitting that he, as the father, had acted abusively. This kind of authentic spirit of love can take families a long way in rectifying misdeeds and restoring the health lost from child abuse.

Older Sister

Chapter 2

Diversity

While one of the original images of the United States was that of a melting pot, America is multicultural. The strength and beauty of diversity in this country is not only overlooked, but often criticized. Appreciation for cultural diversity plays a large role in the healthy development of identity in adolescence within a family structure. Discrimination can be a traumatic experience for teenagers.

Public policy addressing issues of diversity both in the 1990s and historically has created traumatic stress for many young people. Consistent help, such as economic aid or second language instruction is not provided in communities in large enough dosages to include all young people. There is not a consistent mission statement, such as that of the Children's Defense Fund, to "Leave No Child Behind." Even in the most well-meaning communities, differences are exacerbated by the unequal access to resources. From an adolescent perspective, the gaps are dramatic and often seemingly insurmountable.

SOCIOECONOMIC VARIABLES

Economic differences are too great. Teenagers from lower income families have too hard a time trying to keep up with technological advances, good health care, and other aspects of an advanced society. In terms of years of education and job opportunities, young Americans who grow up in homes where parents have incomes of over $100,000 surpass young people coming from homes with parental incomes at or near poverty level. In addition, many incarcerated youths are described as having economically disadvantaged families.

Terri's and Nathan's Stories

Terri, a colleague raised in an upper-class family, told the following story: When she was thirteen, it never occurred to Terri how others her age were living. The summer of her thirteenth year, she spent the first month lying on a raft in the swimming pool in the backyard and the next two months away at a private camp riding horses. By contrast, Nathan, a foster son of the same age, and a former foster son of acquaintances of her family, spent the summer in a receiving home after his adoptive parents changed their minds, relinquishing the adoption. Totally rejected and disenfranchised, he managed to live through the summer months with a pervasive fear of what was to become of him.

Tracy's Story

Tracy spent the summer of her thirteenth year taking care of her two younger siblings while her single-parent mother worked. This young girl played games with her sisters, made their lunches, and also started dinner before her mother returned. Tracy commented how tired she was that summer, and how stressful it was making sure her younger sisters did not get into trouble or harm themselves.

Tommy's Story

In his thirteenth summer, Tommy was running the streets with gangs. His two older brothers, ages eighteen and twenty, were selling cocaine to support themselves. Both had dropped out of school. Tommy remembers being at the scene of an alley fight where another youth was shot and killed. Witnessing this murder was traumatic and changed the course of his life. Now seventeen, he runs the streets, is homeless, and although he works at fast food restaurants, he is unable to support himself. His life is difficult and painful.

The economic structure of our country continues to create undue hardship, again institutionalizing our ambivalent, unresolved conflicts. Nancy Gibbs (1995) wrote, "There may be ten million working poor" (p. 20). She elaborated the repercussions:

As President Clinton likes to note, two-thirds of the nearly forty million Americans with no health insurance live in families with full-time workers. A single illness or injury will plunge a family into crisis. Often health-care concerns override all others in determining whether someone stays on welfare or goes to work. Being poor means making choices: the phone bill or the gas bill? Cough medicine or snow boots? (Gibbs, 1995, p. 18)

So, working in the 1990s may not move a family out of poverty. Young people who drop out of school or have been battling traumatic stress may not have the education to keep up with a better-paying technological market. This population is hard-pressed to find a job in the United States. Economic factors play an important role in either alleviating or exacerbating traumatic stress in adolescence.

The following information is presented not as an exhaustive probe nor as a pragmatic analysis. Rather, it is presented as a catalyst for further thinking and discussion.

What is socioeconomic class? Karl Marx referred to class as an economic stratification between two groups of persons in a capitalistic society—those who control and own the means of production and those who provide the labor but do not control it. The distinction more popularly defined today exists between those who have and those who have not—a segregation between substantial stock and real estate holders and nonholders.

There are many traumatized teenagers who have a foreshortened sense of future. They do not see themselves as real estate holders in the future. They do not see themselves as bankers or lawyers either. Often, young people who have been struggling with trauma and are faced with limited access to economic resources have thoughts such as: "No one with a mop can expect respect from a banker, or an attorney, or men who create jobs, and all you have is a mop. Are you crazy? Whoever heard of integration between a mop and a banker?" (Clark, 1965, p. 2).

Beyond this simple economic differentiation, the concept of class becomes blurred and ambiguous—especially when the two groups become further subdivided, or when an additional group is added. Today, sociologists using both of the former means of derivation have identified a phenomenon called a middle class, a class whose growth Marx did not foresee. This class has been inconsistently defined by both sociologists and by persons who claim to be members of it. Furthermore, ambiguity exists in the definitions of all strata, not just that of the middle class. Two different modes of analysis of class are presented as follows to indicate the apparent inconsistencies.

In their 1949 study of Jonesville, a small city (under 10,000 people) believed to represent a typical midwestern community, Lloyd Warner and colleagues (cited in Gordon, 1963) developed an Index Status Characteristics (ISC) scale based on occupation, income, house type, and dwelling area as a basis for dividing the Jonesville populace into six categories:

> *Upper Class:* Old family money and nouveau rich
> *Upper Middle:* College-educated businessmen, belong
>   to patriotic clubs, e.g., Rotary
> *Lower Middle:* Skilled labor, e.g., plumbers
> *Upper Lower:* Laborers
> *Lower Lower:* Poor people with little education

As Gordon aptly put it, "An important question which must be raised at this point is whether the classes or status groups in the Warner system are meant to be thought of as real entities having a separate and identifiable existence or simply as convenient and arbitrary categories which divide an unbroken continuum" (1963, p. 90). It could be a continuum which may not even apply to ethnic groups.

A second approach to societal stratification to consider is that formulated by Edward Banfield (1990). Banfield developed a theory of societal stratification based on time orientation. He depicted four subcultures as follows:

> *Upper:* Future-oriented. Has a sense of a long life span. Has a sense of social responsibility. Sets long-range goals. Delays gratification.
> *Middle:* Somewhat future-oriented. A person provides for children in the near future only. A person shows less social responsibility.
> *Working:* With a "fixed horizon." A person is more subject to the whims of society than a creative force. Believes he will be old by the time he is middle-aged.

Lower: Present-oriented. Feels helpless, powerless. Events perceived outside control of person.

Banfield (1990) tore away the outer layers of human existence (or social role) in the United States, such as employment and education, and described how important personal vision and motivation are to class structure. Underneath the layers lies the person. President Clinton's vision and sense of social responsibility represent traits of an upper-class member as defined by Banfield. President Clinton earned his education and his position. This vision is not held in all ethnic communities. Developing and maintaining personal bonds or protecting the environment may have higher value or meaning. Assuming that all Americans share the same values not only creates misunderstanding, but it may actually exacerbate traumatic stress symptoms in some people.

IMMIGRATION

There is significant evidence in the last two centuries to refute the idea that the approximately 58 million immigrants who have come to our shores since 1820 have become amalgamated into one homogeneous American culture. It does seem time to reform the sixty-year-old AFDC (Aid to Families with Dependent Children) program, but why discriminate against legal immigrants? Immigrants have often provided a backbone to our economy. Institutionalized ambivalence transcends time. The inscription on the beloved Statue of Liberty, by the poet Emma Lazarus (1883) says, "Give me your tired, your poor, your huddled masses yearning to breathe free, the wretched refuse of your teeming shore. Send these, the homeless, tempest-tost to me. I lift my lamp beside the golden door" (p. 9).

The melting pot theory does not seem to hold true in reality, nor does it seem important for everyone to assimilate and acculturate. First, some social group behavior is characteristically ethnic. Second, there are historical examples in which Americans who claim they have been striving to assimilate immigrant groups into their own framework have worked against their proposed goal. Third, several class theorists have admitted their failings in attempting to incorporate ethnicity into their socioeconomic class frameworks. There is significant evidence to show that ethnic groups in various communities have established lifestyles, goals, and behavior patterns that are inherent to their lineage and often in contrast to the Protestant work ethic ideology. These pockets of humanity have sought to preserve the richness of tradition. When a culture's traditions are threatened by discrimination, both subtle and overt, the end result is often a traumatic effect.

Gans (1962), in his book, *The Urban Villagers,* discussed a community of Italian Americans who lived in the West End of Boston. This book, published in the early 1960s, captured the impending doom of urban redevelopment. Gans depicted the "West Enders" as not terribly interested in education or careers, both of which help lead to prosperity. In fact, they looked down on ambitious businessmen and professionals. For the West Enders, strong familial and peer relationships were what was important in their lives. A job represented only a vehicle for minimal support; it was not a source of primary orientation and gratification. Gans attested:

> Because of the group rejection of middle-class ways, the individual who does wish to seek a career to live in a middle-class neighborhood, and to adapt other patterns of middle-class culture must therefore be able to separate himself from the peer group society. (1962, p. 222)

Gans admitted that, "The West Enders . . . can be conceived as forming a working-class subculture, which differs considerably from both lower- and middle-class subcultures" (1962, p. 230).

Another illustration is that of a Jewish neighborhood on the Lower East Side of New York City. Hutchins Hapgood (1967) depicted the significant sense of Jewishness within this community by describing the prevalence of innumerable, distinctly Jewish newspapers, Hebrew schools, Zionist clubs, and social groups. The sense of community on the Lower East Side is depicted as strong and binding. Ethnic affiliation motivated behavior and at the same time gave meaning to the lives of the Jews. Numerous Jewish newspapers served this community: *Tageblatt,* a daily paper; *Abend-Post* and *Herald,* two weekly journals; *Arbeiterzeitung,* a socialistic journal; and *Vorwarts* and *Abendblatt,* two progressive journals. The Yiddish stage exemplified meaningful entertainment for the neighborhood, with three Yiddish theaters: the People's Theater, the Windsor, and the Thalia.

Hapgood (1967) also explained the strong sense of Russian "Jewishness" in literature with the following examples: poet Eliakim Zunser wrote in Yiddish about the simplicity of his people, while Menahem Dolitzki wrote of a morality that shrouds his race and language; and prose writer S. Libin delved into the sordid atmosphere of the Jewish ghetto, while Leon Korbin added a satirical touch to tenement life.

Both Gans' and Hapgood's books were written in the 1960s, and are wonderful commentaries on the richness and history of ethnic life in this country. Unfortunately, the vital importance of cultural/community heritage is often discounted. Not only has public policy not supported this kind of heritage, it has undermined community traditions:

> When the term community is used, the first notion that typically comes to mind is a place in which people know and care for one another—the kind of place in which people do not merely ask 'How are you'? as a formality but care about the answer. This we-ness (which cynics have belittled as a 'warm, fuzzy' sense of community) is indeed part of its essence . . . Communities speak to us in moral voices. They lay claims on their members. Indeed, they are the most important sustaining source of moral voices other than the inner self. (Etzioni, 1993, p. 31)

Many documented instances of distinctly ethnic prejudice have occurred in the history of this country. The following immigration laws, reported by Higham (1988), hopefully will set the foundation for this argument:

1. In 1798, four laws were passed under the Alien and Sedition Acts. In addition to the Alien Enemy Act were the following: the Naturalization Act, which increased residency requirements for naturalization from five years to fourteen years; the Alien Act, which gave the president the right to expel from the country or imprison immigrants thought to be radical; and the Sedition Act, which, in part, imposed fines and imprisonment if foreigners took too many liberties with freedom of speech and freedom of the press.

2. "No variety of anti-European sentiment has ever approached the violent extremes to which anti-Chinese agitation went in the 1870s and 1880s. Lynchings, boycotts, and mass expulsions still harassed the Chinese after the federal government yielded to clamor for their exclusion in 1882" (p. 25).

3. In 1891, a federal law controlling immigration was passed. All those immigrants who did not meet with U.S. inspection standards were refused entry and sent back.

4. In 1894, the National Board of Trade proposed to limit immigration through the establishment of a literacy test. A bit later in the 1890s, the Immigration Restriction League was formed, led by Harvard graduates. This league devoted its efforts to promoting the literacy test.

5. In 1917, the literacy bill finally was passed. The bill also barred Asians—Hindus and Eastern Indians. It did manage to support Roosevelt's agreement with Japan and allow Japanese to immigrate, provided they could read, and it did provide for other exceptions.

6. In 1918, a law was passed by Congress which allowed the deportation of immigrants who belonged to any organization that advocated revolt, such as the Industrial Workers of the World (IWW).

7. In 1921, the first quota law was passed, based on the 1910 census results.

8. In 1924, a new quota law was passed, based on an 1890 census which included fewer Eastern Europeans. Visas were introduced in this law as a requirement for admittance. This law reneged on Roosevelt's agreement and prohibited Japanese immigration.

The MacNeil/Lehrer News Hour (1994) reported that in Miami, illegal aliens could apply for asylum in America if they could show that they were being persecuted. This report indicated that the backlog of applications would take a century to process. *The News Hour* also reported that Florida was a state that sued the federal government to obtain funding to provide health care, education, and incarceration to illegal immigrants. As political and economic strife continued to plague their homelands, Haitians, Cubans, and Central Americans fled to South Florida. As the influx continued, Miami officials deported immigrants for nonviolent crimes.

Accompanying the immigration laws and largely responsible for them were innumerable organizations, newspapers, and books which were less subtly anti-immigrant, which Higham (1988) referred to throughout his book, *Strangers in the Land.* There was a wave of anti-Catholic groups which feared "Papal Despotism"; among them were the AFL-CIO under Samuel Gompers, the American Protective Association, the American League, and the Order of American Unions. Other, more generalized groups included the Know-Nothing Party, a pre–Civil War group against all foreigners; and the Ku Klux Klan which advocated white supremacy. Books included those by Madison Grant, indicating both that the races would not blend and that immigrants must be barred to keep the dominant group from becoming extinct. Anti-immigrant newspapers included *Missouri Menace,* against Catholics; and Henry Ford's *Dearborn Independent,* against Jews (Higham, 1988).

The rise of eugenic research prompted Professor Francis A. Walker, president of MIT, together with Nathan S. Shaler, a Harvard science professor, and Henry Cabot Lodge, to say that new races were inassimilable—particularly the southeastern Europeans. The growing fear that immigrants would replace the dominant group approached paranoia. To increase fears, Robert M. Yerkes, president of the American Psychological Association, and William McDougall, a social psychologist, propounded that WASPS were a super race with IQs far superior to those of others. Thus immigrant groups became branded with inferiority that was claimed to be ethnically founded (Higham, 1988).

ETHNICITY AND RACE

A newspaper article described the following discrepancies in our country. In 1991, "Black workers earned 77% as much as whites, averaging $18,304; and Hispanic workers made 68% as much as whites, or $16,120 (a slight improvement for blacks but a decrease for Hispanics in constant dollar terms)" (VerMeulen, 1992, p. 5).

Much has been written about whether certain kinds of behavior—both group and individual—may be attributed to socioeconomic class or ethnicity. Most class theorists in the past have not allowed for ethnic differences. They have lumped ethnic groups into the hierarchical scheme based on the Protestant work ethic, i.e., labor, achieve, prosper financially . . . receive the grace of God. Those who have prospered the most reside at the top of the socio-economic class continuum, and those who have not are found at the bottom. This analysis assumes that ethnic groups have been assimilated into the work ethic mode, that ethnic groups have been consciously striving to adopt American culture and American values, that indeed this country has been a cultural melting pot.

With reference to African Americans, the U.S. government has been particularly discriminatory. The Constitution considered an African American as three-fifths of a person in terms of representation. Under slavery, blacks had similar legal rights to other forms of property such as cows and horses—none. They could not own property except at the discretion of their owners, and could not enter into any legal contract, even that of marriage. Clear family boundaries for Black families were destroyed by slavery. In the early 1900s, black Americans were disenfranchised in virtually every Southern state. The *Plessy v. Ferguson* (1896) Supreme Court decision erroneously claimed that separation of blacks from whites implied equality.

Even with the reversal of this decision by *Brown v. Board of Education of Topeka* (1954), young African-American males have had a terrible struggle trying to catch up educationally, and subsequently in the job market. In the *Rocky Mountain News* (1992, June 6), an article appearing under "Economic Indicators" stated, "The jobless rate for black inner-city teenagers is at crisis levels of more than 50% threatening major cities with more violence like the Los Angeles riots, the National Urban League said" (p. 59).

In the early 1960s, marriage laws were ". . . little different from the Nuremberg laws of the Nazis, which prohibited intermarriage between 'Aryans' and the 'inferior' European national groups" (Capitman, 1963, p. 190). Only seventeen states had no interracial restrictions on marriage. Thirty states prohibited marriage between blacks and whites. Sixteen states forbade marriages between whites and Asians, and five states prohibited marriage between whites and Native American Indians (Capitman, 1963). According to Capitman (1963):

Scientifically, it has been clearly established that there is no such thing as a pure race. Yet the courts in states in which marriages between white persons and Negroes in particular are prohibited have undertaken fantastic and sometimes ludicrous efforts to prevent the "contamination" of the blood stream. (p. 191)

The foregoing examples illustrate that as this country was idealistically assimilating and forming a supposed "melting pot," it was setting up incredible institutional barriers to its goal. With such evidence in mind, it may be more easily understood why many class theorists who presuppose the melting pot theory may be largely inaccurate in placing a significant portion of the population of this country in their stratification frameworks.

Of greater importance is that the larger part of the population has wrongly assumed ethnic groups were falling into the scheme of things. In the early 1990s, young African-American males were overrepresented in the prison system. In a Denver detention center in 1993, on a pod of about sixty youths, the authors observed only two white youths. In the late 1990s, "Black children continue to be disproportionately represented by the juvenile justice system—from arrests to courts to secure detention" (Children's Defense Fund, 1996, p. 2). Clearly whites were underrepresented in this situation. Racism and access to resources are possible explanations for this phenomenon.

In American society, traumatized youths, who are often poor as well, endure multiple brands of inferiority just as did the early immigrants to this country. Traumatized young people often carry mental health, criminal, educational, class, and minority status brands. These young people need extraordinary courage to transcend such identity confusion.

Youths from many cultures have struggled with difficult identity issues. Hispanic-American youths may have Mexican, Spanish, Puerto Rican, Central or South American, Cuban, or other roots. Their cultural similarities and differences have not been adequately validated and transmitted intergenerationally in this country. The infamous Bureau of Indian Affairs, rather than building partnerships with American Indian families, often separated children from parents in order to "Americanize" the children. In the latter part of the nineteenth century and through the twentieth century, Native American culture has been inconsistently valued and supported. National origin, language, skin complexion, and social background play salient roles in identity formation during adolescence. The following story is of an African-American youth.

Carlee's Story

Carlee's story is remarkable and her drive to succeed provides an important lesson. When Carlee was fourteen, she was a "perfect" straight-F student, smoking dope, smartmouthing her teachers, and ditching classes. Carlee grew up with consistent psychological abuse. Garbarino, Guttman, and Seeley (1986), in *The Psychologically Battered Child,* referred to the following five areas of psychological maltreatment: corrupting, ignoring, isolating, rejecting, and terrorizing. Carlee grew up in a family where secrets were well kept. One relative had been institutionalized with schizophrenia, an illness the family consistently chose to deny. One of the family members was a batterer and a child molester. Carlee was corrupted by the chemical dependency patterns of several of her relatives. Her primary caretaker was alcoholic, and another relative was a heroin addict. "Creating and sustaining a pattern of behavior that risks permanent social dysfunction (for example, addiction, frigidity, compulsive sexual acting out, or repetitive acts of life-threatening violence) is evidence of severe corrupting" (Garbarino, Guttman, and Seeley, 1986, p. 28).

Carlee was often left without a significant person to approach for guidance. An ignored child usually comes from a family environment where children are not central in importance, or where a primary caretaker is disabled, such as by substance abuse. Ignoring is the essence of neglect.

In her effort to seek companionship and a sense of belonging, Carlee gravitated to a group of street youths, as many young people do in these instances. She grew up in a rough inner-city neighborhood, predominantly black, where many families struggled with drug abuse and pervasive violence, and where raw survival was the main preoccupation. Furthermore, she hated her school. She felt that the teachers did not understand or relate well to their students. The students cut classes and virtually ran wild in the hallways.

When teachers tried to establish order, students often retorted with uncivil and threatening remarks.

Carlee could not visualize herself in a future setting.

Nancy Boyd-Franklin (1989) summarized:

> For poor, urban black families, the task is to help motivate children to achieve and believe in themselves despite the blatant evidence of discrimination that they view every day. For example, young children may see many of the older teenagers in their community unemployed and the evidence of the last hired, first fired policies of the labor market in the widespread unemployment of both teenagers and adults. Many wonder why they should bother to study and go to school if they will end up in similarly hopeless situations. (p. 26)

In tenth grade, Carlee was provided with an opportunity to get out. As part of a high school racial exchange program sponsored by the state, called The Ecumenical Council for Racial Understanding, Carlee moved out of the inner city into an upper-class home in the suburbs until she graduated from high school. She returned home to the inner city on holidays. Her relatives only occasionally ventured out to the suburbs to visit her in these upscale surroundings.

Her new family and school were very different. She now lived in a two-parent home, had all the clothes and material possessions of which she had ever dreamed, and attended a first-rate public high school. Comparing the budgets of the two school districts that Carlee attended, the inner-city district's per-pupil expenditures were one-third of the suburban district's.

Carlee experienced difficult tradeoffs in her new life. She had escaped a traumatic childhood but found herself to be one of a handful of black youths in a mostly white county. She said, "I always felt like an outsider." She maintained that she never sensed she was accepted by her new friends yet felt rejected by her old ones. One of her new friends had said to her, "You dance black, but you talk white." One Halloween, she dressed like a member of the white supremacist organization, the Ku Klux Klan. With revealing black hands protruding from beneath her white robe, she, together with some friends, knocked down figurines of black lawn jockeys that adorned many of the upper-class lawns. Ultimately, she began to believe that blacks were inferior and only lately has derived a sense of what that feeling was all about.

But, despite her pervasive personal doubt, Carlee made remarkable progress. Toward the end of her sophomore year, she had started playing the piano in one of the music rooms after school. Soon after, her new family bought her a piano. For the next two years, she took piano lessons and played as many as three hours a day, often soaking her fingers to be able to keep up with the rigorous practices. The summer of her sophomore year she attended a music camp, where she studied the piano and took voice lessons. At the end of her junior year, she was officially recognized as one of the top high school sopranos in the state.

Carlee's love of music provided a springboard for her self-confidence. Her grades started to improve and by the time she graduated from high school, she had earned a B average, an incredible achievement for one who had a corner on the market for getting Fs. Her suburban high school experience was so different for her—no fights and only minor altercations; the crude language she was used to hearing was barely heard. Most of her classmates went on to college; students at this high school understood that it was expected as a normal course of events.

Carlee was accepted into a very good college in the East on a full music scholarship. She later transferred to a well-known university and graduated with a 3.8 GPA. Her academic achievement was heroic in the context of the hurdles she overcame. School in general, even the last two years of high school and in college, were hard for her even though she did very well. She felt the nagging distraction that she should not be there, assimilating the white culture. It was not the "black" thing to do. It may have been easier for her to compete and protest. At one time she was arrested for being part of a civil rights demonstration that blocked a major traffic intersection. She later wrote, "Competing was okay because I could 'show' whites, but accepting or embracing the culture was taboo." Her African-American friends would object to assimilation. They were back in her old neighborhood—not attending school.

Last, she felt alienated from African-American males. To this day, she is concerned about how black males are going to gain the strength and confidence to compete globally. Particularly when

"Fewer blacks go to college today than ten years ago; more black males of college age are in prison or under control of the criminal justice system than in college" (Steele, 1990, p. 124).

After graduating from college, Carlee sang in a national choir. Wanting to give back to society, she is now a full-time probation officer, a chorus teacher at her church, and a member of the board for a local boys' choir. Today, as a beautiful, accomplished African-American woman, she is proud, and grateful for her opportunity in a different environment. Nonetheless, she is not naive enough to believe that money is the solution for all ailments, least of all her internal struggle.

SEXUAL ORIENTATION

Youths who are questioning their sexual orientations face unique developmental tasks with few guidelines. Young people who find themselves outside the socially accepted definitions of sexual orientation or gender identity experience growing up within a social context that can be quite isolating. The results of such isolation in some circumstances may include suicidal ideation or attempts (Hetrick and Martin, 1987; Hunter and Schaecher, 1987; Saunders and Valente, 1987); violence from within the family, as well as outside of it (Hunter and Schaecher, 1987; Martin and Hetrick, 1988); and social isolation (Hammersmith, 1987; Hetrick and Martin, 1987). Such issues may be further compounded by a previous history of child abuse.

Michael's Story

The following is the story of a young boy who grew up on the West coast. This story of hardship depicts some of the struggles of gay, lesbian, and bisexual youth in an American culture that is often condemning, judgmental, and even dangerous. At no time in his childhood did he have the assistance of helping professionals. When asked what kind of help he needed, he was unable to answer. He commented, "I doubt if I would have accepted help—particularly as an adolescent."

Michael was mostly raised with one older sister and a younger brother. His father left when he was six, taking with him two older siblings by another marriage. The only childhood memory Michael associated with his dad occurred when his father let him come along on his bread delivery route. He remembered being so tired from being awakened at 4:00 a.m. that he slept on the bread racks in the truck.

Michael was never quite certain whether the man he called his father was his birth father. He knew his parents were not married when he was born. But it was not until he was fourteen that he was told by his mother that the father he remembered was a boyfriend of hers, not his birth father. This information was given to Michael because the man reappeared.

Michael's reunion with this man was awkward, as might be expected. The man told Michael that his mother had kept them apart, an explanation Michael never trusted. His time with this man was awful. He remembered him not acting like an adult—he smoked pot. The reunion lasted about two months, then the man disappeared forever.

Life with Michael's mother was crazy. Trying to make financial ends meet, she worked three jobs. She drank heavily and caroused with many men in her free time. Her horrifyingly consistent message to Michael and his siblings was that she would have been much better off without them. Michael confessed that at all times during his childhood, he felt like a burden to his mother.

While she worked three jobs, the responsibility for the children fell at first to the oldest sister. But when she turned fourteen, she was forced to move out because she did not complete assigned chores. Michael, at age eleven, took over caring for his younger brother—cooking, cleaning, getting himself and his brother up for school. At the same time, Mother successfully held jobs as a bartender, a factory worker, and a part-time secretary. With whatever free time she had, she would bring home men to satisfy her needs for drinking companions and sexual gratification. If Michael failed to keep the house clean, he was hit by her hand, a belt, or a kitchen paddle.

It was while he was in the eighth grade that Michael started to fight with his younger brother, who was then ten and refused to do chores. Michael started doing drugs, ditching school, and staying away from home. Because Michael was not complying with her rules, Michael's mother threw him out of the house. After his two-month stay with the man who he had believed to be his father in early childhood, he moved in with his sister, who had previously been thrown out.

His older sister was in a battering relationship. He did not have anywhere else to go. His life became a living hell. His substance abuse became life-threatening and he didn't care. At fourteen he was using angel dust, LSD, mushrooms, and his sister's Valium. He dropped out of school and began to experiment sexually. He had sex with two girls and did not find it exciting. He began to sexually experiment with older boys.

Michael realized he was sexually attracted to boys. With no adult guidance to sort through these experiences, Michael determined he was gay. He began to develop crushes on boys and have sexual relationships with them. Also, at age fifteen, he began to live a street life for money, prostituting himself to older males. Once while he was hitchhiking from one job to another, he was accosted and raped by an adult male. He never told anyone about this incident until he was himself an adult.

By seventeen, Michael had given up prostitution because he had met a young man with whom he wished to live. Before moving out of his sister's, he helped her take care of her son who had spinal meningitis. When the boy died, Michael moved in with the family of his boyfriend, Zach. Zach's parents were amazingly open-minded. His mother was a hairdresser and his father a sheet metal worker. The parents allowed the boys to cohabit in their home.

Zach lived a reclusive life. He mostly stayed at home and watched television. He had also dropped out of high school and did not have a job. Zach's older brother had been killed at age eighteen in an automobile accident. Unlike Zach, Michael took the initiative to go to school to train to become a hairdresser. He believed this was the one environment where he would be accepted. Once he finished his training and began working, Michael and Zach moved out and obtained their own apartment.

Ten years later, the two men still live happily together. Michael is involved in a successful career, the sole support of his family. He has grown into a kind and gentle man.

PART II:
STRUCTURAL CHANGE

This section examines some of the prominent social institutions typically involved with at-risk adolescents. These include child protection, juvenile justice, education, and mental health.

The direction of public policy concerning young people in the 1990s is lacking a mission statement that preserves the human spirit of our young. Without such a mission statement, it is seemingly impossible for the national government to proudly promulgate the next generation as healthy citizens. Statements were made against the use of caning as being an uncivil punishment for an American juvenile in Singapore in 1994, yet in that same year in the United States, girls were being shackled together in an overcrowded detention center, further punishing these youths by placing them in an uncivil environment. Are the institutions and beliefs created as foundation pieces for maintaining democracy and educating the young, in fact violating the civil rights of children and adolescents?

At the very least, the messages given adolescents are unclear. If article after article and statistic after statistic keep being released about the emergency state of many teenagers in the United States, why is there not an effective response? There appears to be great ambivalence about how to respond. Many young people and many families receive equivocal messages.

The staff of an alternative school wrote a grant proposal to the city to develop the public property behind the facility. The students and staff were going to build a sand volleyball court, a garden, a soccer field, and put up a basketball hoop. The homeowners living adjacent to the public land held a special meeting protesting the proposal. The argument of the homeowners was twofold: first, they did not wish teenagers hanging out next to their private property, and second, they believed the development would spoil their prized open-space view. Besides holding the meeting, the homeowners lobbied strongly with city officials to block the request. The proposal was denied.

Should youths be punished or forgiven, particularly when public safety is a concern? An example of the ambivalence around this issue is the withdrawal of an admission offer to Gina Grant by Harvard University. When Harvard accepted Gina, the admissions officers " . . . knew nothing of Gina's past" (Mayer, 1995, p. 43). This young girl, at age fourteen, had been charged with murdering her mother in her home in South Carolina. Gina spent about a year in detention. She was then placed on probation and released into the care of relatives while she completed high school. This bright, attractive girl was admitted to Tufts for the fall of 1995. Is this young girl who murdered an abusive mother forgivable or not?

Teenagers in the foster care system are often given the message that they can be productive and learn how to value their own lives and the lives of others. Yet, when a foster teen is moved from one foster home to another, all of his or her worldly possessions are often loaded into a garbage bag for transport. What message about values does this give an adolescent?

Should the energy of five teenagers walking down the street be feared or embraced? At a gang training workshop, one of the preventions suggested by the gang members was for adults to connect and get to know teenagers, whether they are in a group of five or alone, or whether they are in a mall or on the street. How often do adults take the time to explore what teenagers are doing and connect with them?

Marian Wright Edelman, President of the Children's Defense Fund, pleads that adults "Leave No Child Behind." Many are left, quite purposely, as the institutionalized ambivalence toward teenagers manifests itself in families, communities, states, and the nation. In addition, since many of the youths described throughout this book are involved in multiple systems, it is often unclear which system should step forward to accept responsibility for a young person. Perhaps rather than arguing about whose responsibility a given youth's life is, a philosophical shift could be made societally in which adolescents are seen as the responsibility of all adults. Collaborative work creating partnerships between agencies to meet the needs of a youth would likely be more helpful than expecting a young person to meet the criteria for a given agency. Organizations coordinating wraparound services, such as Kaleidoscope in Chicago, often are successful in providing needed and effective services for youths.

Innocence

Joyce Kennedy

Chapter 3

Child Protection

Where is the aegis for the American child? Child protection is a very complex issue with both dramatic and subtle variables. The more dramatic illustrations include physical and sexual child abuse. More subtle examples include: moving young people from foster home to foster home; permitting young people to walk the streets after dark; saying embarrassing comments about young people; or the following:

> A mother, when interviewed by a reporter, revealed that her youngest birth daughter was struggling in school. The reporter printed this story saying that the youngster had "serious learning problems." The reality of the situation was that the teacher was quite difficult and was asked to leave the school. The girl went on to graduate from both junior and senior high with honors.

This was a subtle form of not protecting the young child, as well as demonstrating how difficult it is to be conscious of, or sensitive to, the needs of children and adolescents. It is imperative that much more effort to protect our children and adolescents from harm be put forward by adults. "Children are not an objective, rational group, they respond to the attitudes and values of the adults supervising them more than to specific techniques used to educate or reform them" (Holloran, 1989, p. 15).

Reviewing aspects of publicly funded child protective services is disheartening. There is a clear difference between advocacy interventions to protect a child or adolescent from harm, and the contrived interventions of adults trying to meet needs for social control,

balanced budgets, and legislated regulations. The former responds
to the needs of youths, the latter to the needs of adults. The former
was begun by Henry Berge, C. Henry Kempe, and organizations
such as the American Humane Association and the C. Henry
Kempe National Center for the Prevention and Treatment of Child
Abuse and Neglect. The latter represents a simplistic, short-sighted
creation of public policy. Unfortunately, "Contrary to popular
belief and the propaganda of organized social work, child welfare
does not have an optimistic record of inevitable progress" (Holloran, 1989, p. 15).

HISTORY OF CHILD PROTECTION

The beginning of the realization of child abuse in this country
occurred with the national helplessness felt in 1874 concerning the
traumatic childhood of Mary Ellen Wilson, an eight-year-old child
found by a New York social worker after having been terrorized by
her caretakers. Mary had been neglected and beaten. Because no
laws existed protecting Mary's rights, police were unable to take
action. Finally, the case was brought to trial by a colleague of Henry
Berge, founder of the Society for the Prevention of Cruelty to
Animals (Gelles, 1996). Mary was placed in an orphanage and her
foster mother placed in jail. In the next year, the Society for the
Prevention of Cruelty to Children was founded. From this agency
evolved the larger umbrella agency of the American Humane
Association. From 1875 to the early 1900s, child protective agencies sprouted under the auspices of foundling hospitals and charity
homes (Zigler and Hall, 1989).

Early history is permeated with examples of children and adolescents viewed as less than the center of the universe. In early biblical
history, Herod ordered the slaying of young males under two years
of age. Roman historical accounts describe unwanted children
being put to death. Certainly, in many written summaries of early
colonial history, adults demanded absolute obedience by threatening to flog young people.

In the United States, with the passage of the Social Security Act
of 1935, struggling families were recognized, but basically for
experiencing economic difficulties, rather than the broader reality

including mental and emotional hardship. Under Title IV-B, child welfare services were created; under Title IV-A, Aid to Families with Dependent Children (AFDC) was established.

The lasting effects of physical and sexual abuse are well documented (e.g., Burgess et al., 1978; Cicchetti and Carlson, 1989; Kempe et al., 1962), as is the lasting devastation of abandonment and neglect (e.g., Bowlby, 1969, 1973; Garbarino, Guttman, and Seeley, 1986). The grandparent paper, "The Battered Child Syndrome," presented by Kempe et al. (1962), started an awakening to the harm inflicted on young people. In 1974, The Child Abuse Prevention and Treatment Act was passed, defining child abuse as the "physical or mental injury, sexual abuse, negligent treatment, or maltreatment of a child under the age of eighteen by a person who is responsible for the child's welfare under circumstances which indicate that the child's health or welfare is threatened thereby" (Cicchetti and Carlson, 1989, p. 46). It was also under this act that the National Center on Child Abuse and Neglect (NCCAN) was established. Finally, in 1975 under President Gerald Ford, Title XX was created, providing money for direct protective services for children and adolescents. The design of these programs was left up to the states.

Even with the attention focused on the maltreatment of children, corporal punishment of an adolescent was upheld by the Supreme Court in *Ingraham v. Wright* (1977). The defendant was a junior high school boy who was paddled more than twenty times by a teacher, causing a hematoma. The case went to the Supreme Court, which held that the boy received due process and that the action of the teacher did not constitute cruel punishment (Cicchetti and Carlson, 1989).

Historical interventions for social control included the auctioning of wayward youths in colonial New England. This intervention scattered young people throughout the countryside to provide domestic and farm labor (Holloran, 1989). The admittance of minors to alms houses provided another means of removing troubled youths from the larger society (Holloran, 1989; Levine and Levine, 1992). This intervention was particularly disturbing since alms houses were originally established for adults who were homeless, had criminal records, or were diagnosed with mental illnesses.

In 1856, Charles Loring Brace created the Children's Aid Society of New York. Out of a desire to remove children from the alms houses, Brace developed an emigration model of youngsters from East to West. He placed ads in newspapers asking for families "out West" to take children. He claimed that he placed approximately 24,000 children by sending them on orphan trains. This intervention saved the state the cost of institutional care (Levine and Levine, 1992). Heading into the turn of the twenty-first century, the cost of institutional care remains a child protection budget concern.

The foster care movement is an often controversial policy of child protection. In the 1800s in Boston, "The traditional placement of socially deviant children in surrogate families was a local voluntaristic solution for individual children" (Holloran, 1989, p. 31). Holloran surmised, "Later critics of the orphan train focused on the sink-or-swim basis of foster home placement in unsupervised, poorly investigated families, affording little or no contact with the child by the child-saver or his own relatives" (p. 49). In reference to the 1990s, Levine and Levine (1992) stated, "Some critics charge that the entire child protection and foster care system is overwhelmed by numbers and in serious disarray. There are a number of lawsuits against social service agencies" (p. 223).

Discrimination continues as a form of social control. There is a litany of data showing the incarceration of young African-American and Latino males. These young people are at risk in overcrowded detention facilities while child protection teams are trying to find residential placements. In the 1800s in Boston, "Racism not only excluded Blacks from private asylums, but it gradually forced a disproportionate number of Black children into public institutions" (Holloran, 1989, p. 142).

Over a century ago, Hannah Stillman founded the Boston Female Asylum. "Black, and illegitimate girls were usually refused by the BFA, as were girls with a criminal in the family" (Holloran, 1989, p. 36). Young girls associated with sexual promiscuity seemed to be dreadfully ostracized even from private psychiatric facilities. Perhaps fear drives the inability in adults to embrace what is real. For positive change to occur, it is vital to relate to young people both authentically, and with a vision that surpasses the limits of fear. If adults are not able to establish these two criteria in working with youths today, professionals will continue not to hear the urgency in the voices of the young. In fact, without hearing, agency leaders will continue to inadvertently establish policy that threatens youths psychologically, and sometimes physically, rather than protecting them.

After the turn of the twentieth century, many states developed programs to protect young people. For example, Levine and Levine (1992) state that between 1910 and 1920, most of twenty-eight institutions in New York City were receiving public funds. Responding to public reality, the Children's Bureau was created. This bureau initiated child abuse reporting guidelines, and created day care programs and maternity initiatives. The medical priority of protecting children from physical child abuse, led by C. Henry Kempe, did not come into play until the 1960s. "The 1960 White House Conference recommended that the states authorize every community to designate a specific agency for child protective work" (Levine and Levine, 1992, p. 218). County departments of social services were put in charge of reporting abuse and protecting children under Title XX, an amendment to the Social Security Act of 1935. Because of the turf conflicts that have been created by the separate mandates of child protection and mental health, a new federal initiative was legislated, Family Preservation and Support Services, in 1993. The Adoption Assistance and Child Welfare Act, in 1980, according to the American Humane Association, ". . . was the first national effort to shift the direction of federal funding away from foster care and toward preventive and family reunification services" (American Humane Association, 1994, p. 1).

This movement, evolving from the early child guidance family therapy initiatives, focused on keeping a family united. Yet, in Colorado, from the years 1985 to 1995, "Confirmed reports of child neglect have doubled" (Shulman, 1997, p. 25). Also questioning this mandate was a *Newsweek* article by Michele Ingrassia and John McCormick, which created quite a stir. The lead subheading read, "Family: Last year, 1,000 abused kids died—though authorities knew that almost half were in danger. Is it time to stop patching up dead-end families?" (Ingrassia and McCormick, 1994, p. 52). Yet, Ingrassia and McCormick documented public policy: "Even in last year's budget-cutting frenzy, Congress earmarked $1 billion for family preservation programs over the next five years" (p. 53). While family preservation programs provide valuable services to many families, there are some families in which the children's needs for protection exceed the adults' right to parent.

The *Newsweek* article tragically described nineteen youngsters found in February, 1994, in a Chicago tenement house. The children shared the apartment with roaches and rats; they fought a dog for his bone; they slept on a filthy floor while the county department of social services gave tacit approval. Ingrassia and McCormick (1994) cited another horrifying example, this one a brutal slaying of a three-year-old boy by his mother. "Even in the most egregious instances of abuse, children go back to their parents time and again" (p. 54). But they do not have to go back. Child and adolescent protection must be prioritized number one and family preservation number two. The following are recommendations for a more effective social service system.

CREATIVE THINKING

Foster parents and caseworkers are significant adults and caretakers for many of America's youth. They are in a position to take the responsibility of keeping children safe. These adults are vital to the ultimate protection of children. Successful foster parents are willing to cooperate with and receive help from professionals. There is a new trend in foster care that supports foster parents partnering with birth relatives, when appropriate, creating a community of invested caretakers. The family life of foster homes is investigated and reviewed. The parents are held accountable by state regulations that are enforced through county supervision. County departments of social service keep records concerning the stability of placement. Knowledgeable foster parents of an adolescent understand they will most likely be parenting a youth who has been traumatized. Successful foster parents are willing to learn the dynamics of bewildered adolescents. Foster parents need to relish and nourish the spirit of a teenager and believe in his or her ability to overcome any obstacle.

The role of a caseworker is a difficult one. This professional is often caught in the maze of different personalities—the social service supervisor, the foster parents, the judge, the biological parents, the guardian ad litem, the probation officer, and the adolescent. The most consistent, yet sometimes difficult stance, is for a caseworker to represent what is in the best interest of the child. This position will not always be in the financial interest of the social service agency. The following story is an example:

Tonia's Story:

Tonia was placed in a foster home because of the substance abuse struggles of both of her parents. Her parents wanted her at home. Tonia was a very good student and wanted to make something of her life. It was the recommendation of the caseworker that it was in the best interest of Tonia to live with the foster family, who could provide energy and support for her growth, allowing frequent visitation with the birth family. The caseworker advocated for this disposition to last for three years. The caseworker's administration allowed the disposition for six months. Several days after Tonia was returned home, she ran away.

An important characteristic of successful foster care caseworkers is their wisdom and degree of involvement with a youth. Referring to the national study of 3,950 youths in foster care in 1977 using a model correlating length of stay in foster care with the number of contacts of the caseworker, Seaberg and Tolley (1986) found that "Caseworkers who are in active contact with their . . . [families] seem to increase the likelihood of greater parental visits. The active contact of caseworkers with their . . . [families] also has been found to be associated with a child's earlier discharge from foster care" (p. 16).

The experience and wisdom of the caseworker is essential to successful foster care. A caseworker needs to have an acute understanding of the struggles of the adolescent and the kind of environment he or she will need to neutralize the conflicts and rise above his or her background. For instance, a caseworker needs to understand that a past history of inadequate dental and medical care may need to be transcended in foster care. This wisdom may be acquired through personal experience, education, or a combination of both.

A successful caseworker needs to understand the commitment of foster parents.

An adolescent can be triumphant and contribute to society in a meaningful way if, in his or her life, there is a significant adult who can dance fast. The caseworker for a teenager must understand the importance of this significant person and help make sure this person exists—even for youths who are age sixteen and older.

SUMMARY

Child protection must come first. Ambivalence related to this issue must be resolved by leaders of public agencies at all levels throughout this country. Once established, models of family therapy, family support, family preservation, and family empowerment can be put in place. Child and adolescent protection includes protection from the risk of physical abuse, sexual abuse, neglectful treatment, and psychological maltreatment. The foster care alternative to family reunification can be a positive experience for young people.

Adults need to have an appreciation of the breadth of the issue of raising healthy children and adolescents. Some may be harmed in more subtle ways. Physical forms of harm are clear. Other forms of harm are not. For example, Levine and Levine (1992) described that in 1880 there were instances of children who were neglected and abused, citing some young people forced into trades as street musicians. Currently, children are placed at risk by not being protected in innumerable ways. The questions regarding child protection need to continue to be asked. Where is the aegis for the American child and adolescent?

the streets

Chapter 4

Juvenile Justice

The cover of Karl Menninger's book, *The Crime of Punishment,* states, "The spread of violence has startled the nation. It flares up ominously and everywhere in spite of our laws and our courts. Or could it be because of our laws and our courts—and ourselves?" Note that his book was published in 1966.

Perhaps one of the biggest challenges in current public policy involves youths who have committed violent crimes. "Adolescent males, constituting only 8 percent of the total population, commit 50 percent of violent crime" (Steiner, Garcia, and Matthews, 1997, p. 357). Even though they are legally still children, society needs to be protected from their violence. The means of providing such protection is at issue, however. In addition, nonviolent offenders may be asking for a different kind of help.

The media have provided dramatic attention to young people in the 1990s. Much of this attention has focused on the criminal acts youths commit.

> The rate of homicide committed by Colorado youth nearly tripled between 1988 and 1991. Thirty percent of teen deaths in 1994 were due to violence (homicide or suicide). Colorado's adolescent suicide rate nearly doubled between 1970 and 1990. (Shulman, 1997, p. 33)

On the cover of *Time,* August 2, 1993, young people were referred to as, "BIG SHOTS: An inside look at the deadly love affair between America's kids and their guns." The cover of *The New Yorker,* September 13, 1993, featured children packing machine guns as they descended from their school bus. In Colorado, on October 7, 1993, a sixteen-year-old boy, Marcus Fernandez, was sentenced to life imprisonment without eligibility for parole. The boy was charged with the murder of Officer Lyle Wohlers. The precedent for life imprisonment without parole has been set in the early 1990s. Some of our young people will spend their entire lives incarcerated. Projected rates of incarcerations of juveniles have been given by the Justice Department, which estimates a 100 percent increase for violent crimes by the year 2010 (Myers, 1995). "The juvenile arrest rate for violent crimes may well double in the next fifteen years, the Justice Department says" (Myers, 1995, p. 2A).

However, in 1995, according to a Children's Defense Fund (1996) report, the rate of juvenile crime in the United States fell:

> What did surge until 1995, prompting serious, legitimate concern, were the rates of juvenile violent crime—particularly gun violence. Between 1985 and 1994, juvenile arrests for violent crimes (murder, forcible rape, robbery, and aggravated assault) rose 75 percent, largely driven by an increase in gun crimes. (p. 2)

Many of these teenagers are struggling with a child abuse trauma syndrome. In a recent study, Steiner, Garcia, and Matthews (1997) stated, "A trauma oriented approach to juvenile delinquents might help us see the human dimension in crime" (p. 364). Additionally, studying the links between trauma and delinquent behavior has important implication for the diagnosis, management, and treatment of juvenile offenders. Such connections would also shed light on the evolving sequelae of post-traumatic stress disorder over time. Child maltreatment is significantly related to post-traumatic stress disorder (PTSD) and delinquent behavior (Steiner, Garcia, and Matthews, 1997). However, juvenile law breakers are frequently given the diagnosis of conduct disorder without assessing differentially for post-traumatic stress disorder. In other words, it may be that the delinquent behavior is a result of child abuse, rather than merely a behavioral disturbance in the young person. Without such a perspective, youths may remain inaccurately identified and horribly mistreated.

A report by the National Advisory Mental Health Council (1993), published in the *American Journal of Psychiatry,* addressed studies and recommendations for treating severe mental illness. This nineteen-page report devoted only one paragraph to the psychiatric needs of children and adolescents. The opening sentence asserted that "Epidemiologic data on the prevalence of mental disorders in the United States are not yet as well developed for children as they are for adults" (p. 1450).

A relationship between child abuse or the violation of a young person's civil rights and mental illness appears to be emerging. Loyola University Chicago School of Law developed a program called CIVITAS or the ChildLaw Center. This center represents the cross training of psychiatry and law students. The law and psychiatry students are encouraged to collaborate on the difficult issues of protecting our nation's children. This perspective represents a macro vision encouraging institutional change. Graduate school boundaries are mitigated as students from different disciplines interface with one another.

The public policy approach to such problems often involves increasing juvenile detention space. This provides only a temporary and insufficient solution. Warehousing youths in detention centers exacerbates their alienation and sense of isolation. The environment of a detention center does not provide a healthy environment. It would be similar to treating a broken bone with numerous Band-aids with sandpaper-like texture.

Traumatic stress experienced by teenagers is related to what is perceived by politicians as youth violence. The 1990s have been riddled with media stories describing real horror. On December 27, 1991, the headline on the front page of the *Rocky Mountain News* read: "Juvenile Violence Surges in Colorado: Murder, assault arrests increase dramatically since mid-80s in state and U.S. Officials fear there is no end in sight." For how long can we endure the stories without being outraged? The front pages of the *Rocky Mountain News,* for the week of September 7 through 11, 1993, headlined the special session of the legislature called by Governor Roy Romer to address the issue of growing teenage violence in Colorado. On September 8, the headline read, "We've got to change: Romer pleads for laws to disarm kids, takes shot at NRA as special session opens." On the next day, the *Rocky Mountain News* headline read, "House toughens gun bill: Law would slap kids with felony, 5 days in jail for illegally having handguns." The stories of teenage violence in Denver reeled from the front pages throughout 1993. One tragic story was the drive-by gang shooting of Broderick Bell, a six-year-old. Another was the murder of retired Judge Spark's sixteen-year-old grandson, Lee Pumroy, shot by a gang member with a semiautomatic pistol. This tragic death propelled the seventy-six-year-old judge back into the political arena as an activist pleading for gun control.

While the legislature was in session, more police scattered throughout the streets of Denver, and neighborhood members congregated to establish night vigils. Many adults perceived that Denver was in crisis during the summer of 1993. Troubled young people with whom we spoke did not perceive a crisis at all.

STORIES OF INCARCERATED YOUTHS

The youths interviewed at the Phillip B. Gilliam Youth Services Center, a Denver detention center, felt that their lives had not changed much for the last eight or nine years. Among them was a nineteen-year-old Blood, a member of the Crimshaw Mafia Gangsters, by his report. He moved to Colorado during his twelfth year. Before the move, he reported that he had gotten into some trouble stealing, but had not committed violent criminal acts. He asserted that he had a hard time with the move, suggesting that whatever anchors he had heaved into place with friends and old neighbors were cut loose. He confided that he had felt "like an outcast" after he moved. This boy's first major arrest was at fourteen for auto theft. His acquaintances in his new neighborhood were gang members. He was beaten up several times and was willing to beat up others. We asked him if he ever had dreams of doing something else. He said, "My dreams are no bigger than my friends." The boy was in Gilliam because he had fired a gun into a group of boys, wounding one of them. He had already spent two years in two different correctional facilities, as well as having run away four times from the same group home.

Two Crips who were best friends were interviewed. They requested that their gang names be used in the book. For their own protection, their names were changed. One of the youths was called Sam and the other Little N. These boys, sixteen and seventeen respectively, were from the Westside Compton Crip, 138th Avenue in Compton, California. The boys had moved from California several years earlier and were involved in selling cocaine. Sam said that all the members of his family were in the 'hood, dealing drugs—this included seven brothers and four sisters by his report. He pointed out that in Compton, many adults are in the 'hood. Sam claimed, "I am not worried about killing people if they are not from my set, not a friend." Then he pulled up his shirt to show us three separate scars where he had been shot.

Little N was facing a year of mandatory incarceration followed by parole. Not showing concern, he affirmed that many of his friends were in the detention system. He bragged that he would not stop breaking the law, and if the law let him out he would probably get rearrested. He also avowed that he would not stop carrying a gun despite the new gun control laws: "You are not safe in the 'hood without a strap."

Little N was asked what he thought of education. He said that the school at Gilliam was "a sorry school." But he went on to say that he never liked school, that he was never able to concentrate. "I worried about proving myself and I worried about my family members," he admitted with a sad countenance.

Last, Little N was asked if he had thought about leaving the gangs. He confessed that he had attended one local group meeting of GRASP (Gang Rescue and Support Program), but had found too many Bloods attending and would not return. He affirmed that he felt safest in the detention center.

A fifteen-year-old girl who was interviewed was in Gilliam because of some tragic circumstance, as the boys sitting around her charged, but she would not speak directly about her life. She did allege that she had been in a residential treatment center for two years before being arrested and the treatment had not helped her. She talked quite a bit about the treatment facility saying that every time she did something wrong, the staff locked her in a seclusion room. She said the experience was "not real."

One of the supervisors at the detention facility stated that the backgrounds of most of the girls in Gilliam were riddled with sexual abuse. The one girl in Gilliam charged with murder was known to have endured incest.

Two Mexican-American boys were also interviewed. One was a member of HUD (Hispanic United Denver Style), and the other, named Shick, was a member of the GKI (Gallant Knights Insane). Shick had been fighting his way into adolescence since age ten. By his report, he had been physically beaten by his mother and placed in foster care when he was a child. His dad was a habitual criminal, whose latest arrest was for armed robbery. Shick had been picked up for assault, auto theft, criminal escape from Gilliam at an earlier time, and burglary. "I have been locked up so many times that I don't care. I am used to an institutionalized life," Shick said. He claimed that all of his family members were part of the GKI and that he had already stabbed someone. He was seventeen.

The other Mexican-American youth was eighteen. He had a total jail time of two years, but the jail time had not deterred him from gang activity. His parents were in the gang, running drugs. Burglary, assault, and possession of drugs were his charges. He had been selling drugs since he was eleven. His relatives sold drugs on his street corner while he watched. Having carried a gun for all of his teenage years, he assured us that guns were easy to come by in pawn shops. He said that he had both purchased a gun and stolen a gun from a pawn shop. We asked him if he thought that something might have helped him as he grew up. He said that he needed to live in a different neighborhood. He talked about the wealthier Anglo neighborhoods (naming them specifically). He said that those kids turned out okay.

Other youths joined the specific young person interviewed. Common themes included parents of these young people abusing drugs and moving. The changing of residences was easier for the youths when they were in the 'hood. Immediately, they could establish a sense of belonging. These youths were bonded to their gang members. Many of them had a history of being bailed out of jail by their friends, unfortunately to be rearrested. But often this was not all bad—they still had incarcerated friends. These youths presented like military fighters, like lost liberation rebels—their violent behavior was part of their culture. Unfortunately, politicians voting to increase detention beds are voting to increase the momentum of this young culture of violence.

Once a child or adolescent is incarcerated, protection of the child is seen as secondary to the protection of society from the youths. While there are instances where a youth may be a serious threat to society if not closely monitored and supervised, there may be more productive ways to meet the needs of society's protection, as well as the growth and development of the youths. Additionally, the impact on incarcerated youths' development will likely be compromised, perhaps endangering society further when they are eventually released.

Detention centers throughout the United States are replete with teenagers who have high-risk symptoms from the traumatic stress of child abuse. A recent study of delinquent youths in the care of the California Youth Authority found that "The PTSD-positive delinquents were clearly the most troubled in terms of impulse control and control of aggression. Such a finding has implications for recidivism" (Steiner, Garcia, and Matthews, 1997, p. 363). Tragically, in the same study, delinquent youths were described as follows:

> Most PTSD-positive youths struggled with the recognition of how deeply events had affected them; most had not revealed their symptoms to anyone despite pronounced interference with functioning (such as intrusive thoughts preventing work during the day and . . . reliving of events to the point of psychotic delusions of the dead person speaking to them; in one case, these delusions led to a hanging). (p. 361)

A highly structured authoritarian model, including a detention system, reformatory, and boot camp, addresses only part of the problem. Consistent structure does not have to be created through authoritarian, disengaged relationships. These youths need powerful, nurturing connections with adult leaders. Adults are afraid of the chilling insensitivity of some young people. Some of the youths who are detained commit terrifying and inhumane acts, such as shooting and stabbing co-workers or robbing and murdering neighbors. Many of these violent offenders are psychologically numb. Incarceration will not likely strengthen their hearts or help them heal.

A youth must form tender feelings toward another human being in order to correct violent behavior. Even a youth who is apt to be biochemically triggered toward aggressive behavior needs a human connection to help him or her learn to control his or her biology. Other examples of young people committing violent acts include youths who have been taught by adults that violence is a viable response to feeling threatened; these youths have developed a value of entitlement to do whatever they want. Another group of youths is thrill-seeking, giving little thought to the outcome of their behavior—searching for a high. The problem of youth violence is multidimensional. These youths need a comprehensive corrective lifestyle, not another inhumane one. These youths need their hearts strengthened. The dosage of medicine society is providing and the form in which it is being administered is not working.

An apt analogy follows. A beloved Newfoundland dog's ear became infected and the dog was in excruciating pain, similar to the pain society experiences with the infection of teenage violence. The owner took her pet to a prominent veterinarian who prescribed a little bottle of medicine, instructing her to put five drops in the dog's ear for several days. A week later the infection was worse and the dog was howling in pain. Rather than go back to the same veterinarian, the owner called a veterinarian who worked at the zoo. The zoo doctor, after seeing the dog, recommended the following: He would prescribe a similar medicine for the next two weeks, but he would prescribe fourteen good-sized bottles of medicine. He asked the owner to pour an entire bottle of medicine in the dog's ear each day. He also prescribed an ointment to rub gently on the dog's ear where the dog had been rubbing the skin. His explanation was that the dog's ear canal was large and needed much medicine. He changed the medicine, thinking that the dog might respond better to a different medicine, and said to administer it for two weeks. In addition, the roughness around the ear needed to be soothed. After three or four days, the big dog was feeling relief. Our youths need much more medicine, often different medicine, and soothing ointment applied by caring adult leaders for a longer period of time.

If adults tightly structure the life of a young person who has yet to master the burden of freedom, how is he or she going to learn? When the struggle with the burden of freedom is taken away because the stakes are too high, the wrong medicine is being used. Many young people, even most violent ones, can and will develop inhibitions and empathy in stages, if given appropriate guidance. For many young people, their freedom is taken away for inordinate periods of time, the development of internal inhibitions and empathy is not necessary to either their survival in their current situation or in their anticipation of release. Most incarcerated youths are not imminently dangerous. Better assessments of incarcerated youths must be made. Community safety must remain a priority of juvenile justice, but not by scapegoating misunderstood teenagers.

Studies have shown over and over again that locking up youths does not consistently help them. According to Ginzberg, Berliner, and Ostow (1988):

> The institutionalization of young people in medical [psychiatric] centers, drug detoxification units, jails and prisons is often highly dysfunctional as far as their future development is concerned. Individuals with low intelligence as well as limited schooling are a disproportionately large part of the institutionalized population. Because most public facilities operate at or above capacity, they seldom have the resources required to provide any significant amount of rehabilitation. Accordingly, when the confined are released they return to their old haunts and slip back into their former ways. (pp. 35-36)

Any connection with an adult leader is terminated forever, and the young person is now expected to handle his or her life without the formerly provided feedback. But if a young person keeps returning, the message from the young person may be that he or she needs more help and more time, not that he or she needs another punishment.

Time is often ambiguously interpreted in our thinking about impacting troubled youths. Some adults feel that careful organization of time in rehabilitation services is imperative. Most adults have sat through lectures where teachers have repeated themselves over and over again, wasting time, or conversely, have skimmed issues that need to be considered for longer periods of time. One of the dilemmas in correcting behavior is that punishment is determined by a crime and is not determined by the learning curve of the young person. The learning curve, or the time it takes a young person to learn, must be a driving factor in rehabilitative design. Arbitrary ten-day or ninety-day rehabilitation periods may be meaningless to an individual youth.

Recidivism is unfortunately too often the outcome of incarceration. In a Florida study cited by Ira M. Schwartz (formerly administrator of the U.S. Department of Justice Office of Juvenile Justice and Delinquency Prevention), 60 percent of the young people reoffended within a year. In another study in California, 80 percent of the young people were rearrested over a ten-year period (Schwartz, 1989, p. 51).

In his book, *The Child Savers,* Peter Prescott (1981) admitted, "The institutions set up by our society to protect and rehabilitate children in trouble are in fact little better than instruments of their degradation and abuse" (p. 178). Yet, in many states, the detention system has expanded in the last five years—more beds have been added, but not enough. Steve Lipsher (1993) reported in *The Denver Post,* "In a controversial move that critics say could break up families, Colorado's Division of Youth Services is preparing to ship a handful of juvenile lawbreakers out of state in an effort to ease crowding in state detention centers" (p. 4B). In addition, the out-of-state facility is described as charging less per day for each youth than the local Lookout Mountain Youth Services Center, which costs the state $150 per day or $55,000 per year for each youth detained (Lipsher, 1993). Lookout Mountain offers innovative, long-term therapeutic programming to juvenile offenders and is a postadjudication facility. The out-of-state facility, Glen Mills Schools, is more similar to a boarding school model, another model showing promise for juvenile offenders.

In his book, *The Crime of Punishment,* Karl Menninger (1966) reprinted a letter by a father whose three-and-a-half-year-old girl was murdered by a fifteen-year-old boy. The father, rather than seeking revenge through the juvenile justice system, asked the people of Philadelphia to help the boy. The father was concerned that the adolescent boy had been cheated out of love and the healthy development of his soul (p. 198).

There were nearly 2,500 juvenile courts in the United States in the early 1990s (Riley, 1992, p. 48). From speaking with probation officers throughout the country, the court officials agree that teenagers being brought into juvenile courts are younger and bolder. These youths are also accused of committing more violent crimes. And, in Colorado, "Minorities account for 50 percent of juveniles sent to detention, although they comprise only 23 percent of the general population" (Amole, 1991, p. 7).

Ira M. Schwartz (1989) reiterated similar themes: "The rates of serious juvenile crime are high and should not be trivialized. However, we are not in the midst of a juvenile crime wave" (p. 26). Interestingly, he pronounced that, "Teenagers are more likely to commit crimes of violence against other teenagers" (p. 28). And, one of his descriptions of the issue of minority incarceration reads, "The fact that minority juvenile offenders are at greater risk of being apprehended than white youth who commit similar crimes is more than likely one of the critical factors accounting for the extraordinary high rates of incarceration of minority youth" (p. 47).

The original paternal nature of juvenile justice has dramatically failed the ethnic minority populations. It has been historically inconsistently defined in terms of the entire juvenile population. Sadly, "Throughout its development, the juvenile court has been hinged far more on an individual justice approach than an equal justice construct" (Rubin, 1985, p. 18).

One lesson taught in the Talmud was that prepubescent Jewish youths were not subject to corporal punishment. Capital punishment under Moslem law was reserved mostly for adults. And in both Roman and Saxon law, the stage of puberty was especially recognized (Bernard, 1992, pp. 28-29). During the nineteenth century in England, courts of equity were developed to address the needs of children. These courts, also referred to as English courts of chancery were founded in the doctrine of *parens patriae*, by which the king, a chancery judge, or a chancellor provided equitable interpretation of a child's past legal infraction. Youth offenders were called delinquents to protect them from the label "criminal." Lastly, civil courts and other courts of law were founded, providing more rigid interpretation of rules. When translated into U.S. law, juvenile proceedings were civil, not criminal (Davis, 1974, pp. 2-3). As of 1996, in Colorado, a juvenile as young as twelve who is accused of murder can be tried in an adult court.

As the juvenile justice system developed in this country, it became more and more intertwined with social welfare systems, and as a result, the judicial process became increasingly vague and confused (Davis, 1974, p. 4). In his book, *The Child Savers,* Prescott (1981) wrote "I am . . . writing here about wasted lives, destroyed lives and an institution set up by society to ease grief and pain but which inadvertently—helplessly, knowingly—increases anguish" (p. 8).

This institution creates anguish for some court officials as well. In Atlanta, Georgia, Judge Glenda Hatchett, who presides over juvenile court, has an inside perspective. "As she sits on the bench overlooking one of the nation's busiest juvenile courts, Glenda Hatchett has an unencumbered view of two of the nation's most pressing ills, juvenile delinquency and child abuse" (Thomas, 1996, p. 6). The burdens of her job are tremendous, as exemplified by a horrific tale, which she heard seven years ago as she began her career, of three-year-old twins who were "pummeled" by their father with his fists:

> She hurried away from the bench to a private bathroom in her chambers and dropped to her knees in prayer, "God, please give me the strength to move my energy from grieving and to use my energy to try and figure out what to do for the children you put before me." (Thomas, 1996, p. 6)

In the early 1800s in this country, what was established to protect wayward youth was a network of houses of refuge. "The House of Refuge was a slightly modified version of the old and well-established method for handling pauper youths in the past—put them in an institution for a period of time and then apprentice them out to rural areas where they work on farms until they become adults" (Bernard, 1992, p. 75). Interestingly, "The term 'juvenile delinquent' originated with the idea that these youths were potential paupers, and the term itself conveys that meaning" (Bernard, 1992, p. 157). The acknowledgment of public policy has been to create residential institutions focused on tight structure to teach proper work ethics (Bernard, 1992, p. 158). The first detention center was created in 1824. The center evolved as a supposedly more civilized New York refuge house—protecting young people from adult prison. Youths were locked up at night, at times commanded to be silent, and worked two hours in school and eight hours on a job (Prescott, 1981, p. 53). Unfortunately, "The few children who were so confined were not reformed" (Prescott, 1981, p. 54).

Nationally, some of the stories of incarcerated adolescents are horrifying: our young people are sexually assaulted, kicked, beaten, isolated for weeks in seclusion rooms, handcuffed to window bars, placed in straitjackets, and left in cells with flies, spiders, blood, food, and spit smeared on the walls (Schwartz, 1989, pp. 12-13).

Two historical state supreme court cases clarified the acute judicial dilemma for young people that are still cited today by attorneys for juveniles. The first was the case of Mary Ann Crouse: in 1838, the Pennsylvania Supreme Court ruled that *parens patriae* of the court could supersede the deprivations in development caused by Mary Ann staying in the home. Mary Ann was to stay at a refuge house (Bernard, 1992). In the second case, the Illinois Supreme Court ruled in 1870 that Daniel O'Connell could not be held in a refuge house on the legal grounds he would grow up in a disadvantaged setting. Even though the pauper home life of Daniel would be bleak, this world would be better than a more restrictive setting (Bernard, 1992).

The issue of whether or not teenagers should be placed out of their homes has disguised the larger issue of too few homes and often poor placement choices for youths. There is a paucity of loving homes and there are too many underfunded and unimaginative residential treatment centers. Furthermore, most of the treatment facilities supported by public funding provide time-limited stays. Continuity of care is often not available.

The boarding school is an institutional model that has been a cornerstone in the development of successful people for centuries. Such a model could be adapted for traumatized youths. There are residential institutions for adolescents today that are highly successful and safe, provide wonderful status for teenagers, have established structure, and are staffed with loving adult leaders. Many young people with backgrounds of trauma and delinquency have successfully attended these institutions. Although such institutions are expensive, they are less expensive, as a whole, than residential placements already established for delinquent youths. These institutions are more popularly referred to as prep schools or boarding schools—Choate, Exeter, Andover, amd Kent, to name a few of these U.S. schools. Although these schools are designed for high-achieving, young people who have grown up for the most part in privileged backgrounds, these institutional models could be modified to serve delinquent youths.

With such excellent residential models already in place for young people, it is disconcerting that so many public policy makers have not reviewed the strengths and applicability of these institutions for young delinquents. Nationally, several creative models exist, such as Glen Mills Schools in Delaware County, Pennsylvania. There are family and neighborhood stresses from which young people need to be protected. Staying at home in the least restrictive setting may not always be in the best interest of the youth. The prep school model would demand that the staff relating to juveniles be well-educated, and optimistic for all young people. There does not seem to be a downside to new thinking; Schwartz (1989) stated, "Some people argue that the problems with the juvenile court are so severe and deep-rooted that it should be abolished" (p. 160).

Even with ideal residential placement options for young people in trouble with the law, the concept of "due process" to get them into a helpful placement would need to be addressed. The problem of due process came about because the juvenile courts did not want to subject young people to the rigors of a jury trial and other more formal court proceedings. The concept of *parens patriae* tends to interfere with due process, particularly when the rights of parents and the stigmatization of adolescents are considered. Of note is the fact that the first juvenile court was established in 1899, and it was not until 1964 that the notion of due process was legally disputed in relation to young people. In Arizona, Gerald Francis Gault, age fifteen, was picked up on a complaint from a neighbor accusing Gerald of making obscene remarks over the telephone. Gerald received a six-year incarceration sentence. The Supreme Court of the United States ruled that this decision was too arbitrary and did not provide rehabilitative opportunities for the youth. As part of the ruling, six due process rights were granted, as the right of a young person to have counsel and the right to have protection against self-incrimination (Prescott, 1981, pp. 71-73).

According to Judge Polier, who sat as a family court judge for thirty-eight years during the middle of this century, "Few youths in the ghettos won a new lease on life through due process. In court one could sense the bitterness of parents and of youth hurt by discrimination that dominated every aspect of their lives in school, in seeking work and on the streets—left unnoticed by the court and counsel" (Polier, 1989, p. 12).

Despite the efforts of U.S. Supreme Court Associate Justice Abe Fortas and others, the inconsistencies in juvenile justice remain dramatic. For instance, in some states, young people accused of homicide are tried in criminal courts (Bernard, 1992). In some states juveniles, not protected by the concept of *parens patriae*, may be tried for other crimes, such as arson and rape. The Constitution does not mandate that juveniles be tried by juries; the 1971 McKeiver decision upheld this (Rubin, 1985).

Other states are more protective, assigning *guardians ad litem* (GALs; personal court-appointed guardians) to help juveniles stay out of criminal courts. However, even when a guardian ad litem is assigned, many youths are not able to have contact with him or her on a regular basis due to the overburdened system. The probation system has evolved as a system of diversion for young people from the more hardened delinquent path. Probation intake workers commonly put together predispositional hearing reports and work to link their young people with treatment resources in the community. Probation departments sort through the dual system of charges against young people—the status offenses and the delinquent offenses. Status offenses are those that are relevant to the status of minors in this country, such as truancy, curfew violations, and legal drinking ages (Bernard, 1992).

Architecturally, the structure for the juvenile justice system nationally seems to have skeletal inconsistencies. Some states have a statewide juvenile court system, others have juvenile courts as part of family courts or district courts, and some states have a county system of juvenile courts. Juvenile justice responsibilities are nationally consistent, with the exception of minors driving cars and committing violent crimes. Traffic infractions may be addressed in traffic courts, and violent crime cases may be tossed into criminal courts. Otherwise, delinquency status offenses—related to supervision issues and dependency/neglect issues—are addressed by juvenile courts. Sadly, "Judges, on the firing line, tend to be more concerned with the control of delinquency, though they often explore with a juvenile what factors led to the commission of the offense" (Rubin, 1985, p. 16).

The idea of supervision of teenagers has always challenged adult thinking. In the second half of the 1970s, there was a dimension of juvenile court in Colorado called CHINS (Child in Need of Supervision). Nationally there were other acronyms: MINS (Minor in Need of Supervision) and PINS (Person in Need of Supervision). This appeared to be part of the movement to provide correctional programs under the 1974 U.S. Juvenile Justice and Delinquency Prevention Act. The dismal truth turned out to be that, "The Juvenile Justice and Delinquency Prevention Act of 1974 has had little impact on reforming the juvenile justice system" (Schwartz, 1989, pp. 16-17). The artificial nature of the concept of correction remains today. The American Correctional Association at one time searched the country for a model program. "After a lengthy review process, which included on-site visits to the facilities, the experts were unable to find one large youth correctional institution that they felt could be held up as a national model" (Schwartz, 1989, p. 61).

CREATIVE THINKING

Youths need to be supervised, but most through nonjudiciary, community-based options. Some states have worked very hard at developing different kinds of programs ranging from intensive tracking and home-based models of intervention to intensive residential treatment models. Mental health center clinicians are often asked to consult by providing prescreenings or psychiatric assessments. These assessments are complex and need to be thoughtful and comprehensive. Basic issues of importance are: How much protection does the youth need? How much protection does the community need from the youth? What is the youth's ability to monitor or regulate his or her own responses to life? What are the stresses on the youth? What are the youth's capacities for self-healing? What resources have been tried? Why have the prior interventions been helpful or unhelpful? Then the questions go beyond the delinquent act. How extensive are the numbed-out feelings of a young person, for example, following the burglary of a private home by gang friends? What is the history of child abuse of a boy who pulls a knife on another boy at school? Why did a boy, on acid, steal his father's car?

The petition plea process—in which a youth can admit or not admit to a petition, as opposed to the guilty/not-guilty bargaining process—provides a hopeful, respectful choice for youths. The concept of restitution through community services—for young people who commit infractions that adversely affect others in the community—is often corrective.

An interesting reform would be to separate all nonviolent actions of young people from the justice system, and to place supervision of these youths within a state government-sanctioned system of state-certified mentors and advisors in offices in each community. The system would be designed to provide young people with a stable, energetic, humane infrastructure of adult professionals serving their own communities. The court system would be eliminated in nonviolent offenses. After all, Prescott (1981) boldly stated, "All the studies and statistics have demonstrated that exposure to a court does a child more harm than good" (p. 239). Instead of a court, there would be a department of the state called the Office of Adolescent Development and the office would be staffed by both adult and adolescent community leaders. All juvenile residential structures would copy the excellent standards of some of the preparatory school models. The model, of course, would have to be adapted to the needs of repeat offenders. How much and where these models would need to be modified cannot be learned until tried.

Polier (1989) stated, "Noncompliant youth—whether subjects for exile, for criminal punishment or juvenile justice—have been in the eye of social and political storms throughout recorded history" (p. 19), and, "Court procedures . . . [do] not invite seeing behind the masks worn by delinquent youth" (p. 21)—particularly if the masks are covering up years of traumatic stress.

Justin's Story

Justin's life is highlighted to illustrate his courage and his uncanny ability to take the best from poorly coordinated systems.

At age thirteen, he was picked up for the first time on a felony menacing charge: he was threatening another youth with a knife. Justin admitted to us that he was scared to death of what the juvenile justice system would do with him. He spent a day in detention and was released to his parents the same evening on a $1,000 personal recognizance (PR) bond. There was a preliminary hearing within seventy-two hours, and a court date was set within a month. In juvenile court, he was placed on probation. Justin did not seem to think that this was a bad outcome for him, and when we asked why, he responded, "Why not? Friends will think I am cool."

Probation for Justin was a disaster. He violated one stipulation after another—staying out past curfew, trespassing, being truant. But underneath his behavior, his family had disintegrated and he was not up to handling the suffering. His parents divorced. The efforts of the two parents to mitigate the stress as they tried to make their separate ways were unrecognized by Justin. He finally started to run away from each of his parents' homes. When he was picked up, the police would place him in a holding cell and ask for his name, Social Security number, and his date of birth. The first several times he was picked up for running away, the police released him to his parents. When Justin's actions were looking more habitual, his probation officer was called and finally he was taken to detention again. Within seventy-two hours a hearing was held. He had an advocate in court, his guardian ad litem (GAL) who had been assigned to him after the first several runs. He described his GAL as a nice, middle-aged woman who would recommend whatever he wanted. He wanted runaway allegations to be deferred. Even with the runs deferred, where would he live? The recommendation of his probation officer was for him to be placed away from his parents in foster care. Placement did not help because he ran from foster care to the home of one of his parents. He also started abusing drugs and manifested continued assaultive behavior. Efforts were made by the court to provide family counseling, drug counseling, individual therapy, and day treatment for this young man. All efforts were to no avail. Finally, he acquired so many violations of his probation that he was sentenced for one year to a juvenile correctional institution, where treatment and education were offered. He was not warehoused under despicable conditions. He said that what helped was not the punitive nature of the institution, but the educational opportunities. He said that he was asked to read regularly, and along the way he was taught a way of looking at day-to-day life from more than one perspective. He explained to us that he believed one's initial thought was the first perspective and a counterthought was the second. An example given by Justin was, "Let's say someone calls my mom a name. The first thought that enters my mind is, hit the kid. The counterthought that enters my mind is, this kid doesn't know my mom, why bother?"

Justin is currently eighteen, working full-time, living on his own, and about to return to high school. His rehabilitation came from the education he was provided in a correctional institution. The setting of the institution was not the best. However, it is interesting to speculate about the importance of education in general and the role it plays in neutralizing deviancy. And this notion certainly supports Polier's (1989) statement, "Greater justice for youth cannot be separated from America's policies and practices that affect all youths in this country" (p. 163), as with education, discussed in detail in the next chapter.

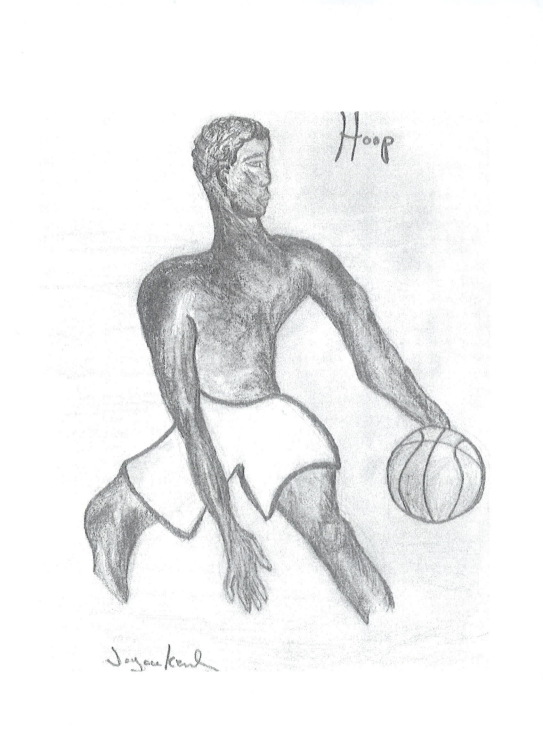

Hoop

Chapter 5

Education

In U.S. public schools, troubled and disadvantaged youths are often stigmatized and inadvertently humiliated by the system that is attempting to provide them with needed services. This can occur when professionals working to correct behavioral and learning problems in these youths must assign state-mandated labels to identify youths in special education classes. For example, some of the labels currently being used in Colorado include the following: SIED (Significant Identifiable Emotional Disability); SIEBD (Significant Identifiable Emotional or Behavioral Disability); SLIC (Significant Limited Intellectual Capacity); PCD (Perceptual or Communicative Disability); and MD (Multiple Disabilities) (from the Colorado State Board of Education, Department of Education, Colorado Code of Regulations 301-8; "Rules for the Administration of the Exceptional Children's Education Act," 1992: cited in Long and Chapman, 1996).

These labels are not all-inclusive, and thus professionals often do not take into consideration a young person's background, that may include years of experiences such as protecting a mother from her alcoholic and abusive partner, or enduring a long history of emotional neglect due to parental substance abuse. The adolescent often sees these labels on his or her Individual Educational Program (IEP) records, and is sometimes asked for a signature if they are of a certain age. The next agency that becomes associated with the youth reads and accepts the labels on faith. The teenager becomes stigmatized and finds it hard to get free of these records. Ironically, these young people need to have such labels in the current system of education in order to obtain the special services they need. The reality is that many young people need extra support educationally, but is it the right kind? The chilling data that indicates, "Roughly half of the U.S. prisoners are high school dropouts" (Shulman, 1997, p. 28), speaks to the need for educational reform.

The educational needs of these youths are complex. Young people who have lived with chronic abuse and neglect often have not developed the strength of discipline to learn logical and methodical thinking patterns. They often have not learned structured thought processes, but instead have developed a hypervigilant, easily distracted cognitive approach to intellectualizing which serves them poorly in problem-solving situations. Further, the trauma of child abuse can impair the ability to form trusting relationships, a necessary element for accepting or trusting the knowledge imparted by the teacher.

When the essential support that should come from families is weak, the school often becomes the ship that carries the young people on board, providing them with the opportunities to change the courses of their lives. Public Law 94-142, or the Education for All Handicapped Children Act of 1975 (renamed in 1990 as The Individuals with Disabilities Education Act) emphasized specific needs by requiring IEP). It seems, however, that this act has more advantage for physically handicapped youth and less for emotionally disabled teenagers. The act failed by neglecting to validate the heroism of traumatized young people. The survival skills of these youths are not recognized. Too often the suffering of this young generation is not acknowledged. Teenagers need to tap this courage and strength in order to discipline their minds for academic growth. A youth who has grown up in a threatening and chaotic environment should not be made to feel intellectually inferior to another youth who has been reared in surroundings that have nurtured intellectual pursuits.

There has been a plethora of educational concerns related to young people as the United States has prepared to move into the twenty-first century. In the early 1990s, many school administrators in Colorado lobbied for legislation to exclude some acting-out teenagers from their schools, rather than redesign schools to meet the needs of all of their districts' youths. With mounting criticism concerning the quality of education and safety in Colorado schools, lawmakers introduced two bills in 1993: the first bill permitted a school to place a youth in a program outside the school if the youth jeopardized the safety of others; the second allowed a school to expel a student charged with a violent crime and place the burden of finding an alternative program on the parent. These legislative pieces were called, "Bad-Kids Bills" (*Rocky Mountain News*, 1993, February 6). A front-page headline in the *Rocky Mountain News* (1992, January 31) reported that in Denver, "21% of the Class of 1991 Quit." By 1994, the drop-out rate for Denver public schools had grown worse rather than better.

In Colorado, there is strong evidence that the educational needs of African-American children are not being well met. The Colorado Children's Campaign (1994) produced a valuable pamphlet titled *KidsCount in Colorado 1994*. In it, Colorado Department of Education statistics showed that from 1991 to 1993, the graduation rate for African-American students decreased from 69.7 to 68.8, while the Anglo-American rate increased from 82.4 to 84.0. In addition, "The gap between the average scores on both the SAT and ACT for students of different racial and ethnic groups has widened over the last five years" (p. 24). A 1992 article elaborated on an eighth-grade national test where less than a fourth of the black students taking the test were able to complete the problems (Morson, 1992). In 1993, African American students made up 5.7 percent of the total student population in Colorado; however, they represented 10.5 percent of the student dropout rate (Colorado Children's Campaign, 1994).

In Colorado public schools, "Black and Hispanic students continue to score lower than White students on tests of academic achievement and are less likely to graduate" (Shulman, 1997, p. 29). Additionally, "About one-quarter of Colorado high school students will drop out before they graduate" (Shulman, 1997, p. 28).

Toward the middle of the twentieth century, an approach to rectify this discrepancy was to move toward having schools become "[agencies] . . . of social adjustment for all American youth" (Ravitch, 1983, p. 11). With this theme of progressivism through the 1960s, schools created more idealism than practical programming. Many curricula lost rigor. Young people often moved from one grade to another without acquisition of needed academic skills. "By 1975, when the College Entrance Examination Board announced that scores on its Scholastic Aptitude Test had fallen steadily for a decade, experimental programs were on the defensive" (Ravitch, 1983, p. 255). The necessary academic standards to achieve entrance to both undergraduate and graduate school seemed to have been nationally compromised.

However, there continues to be an ongoing debate on the validity of the SAT. "The SAT is a voluntary test and each year is taken by differing types of students, which means that its aggregate results are not valid for judging the performance of American schools" (Berliner and Biddle, 1995, p. 35).

Clamoring in the background, citizens propounding traditional education are blaming the progressives for educational failures. The emphasis of classical education is on stimulating intellectual functioning by teaching cultural heritage and knowledge. The vehicles of classical learning are reading and teacher-centered classrooms (Ravitch, 1983). But this educational philosophy has been historically criticized as elitist. Not all young people are visual and auditory learners.

In the early 1990s, educators at Hampden Academy, a day treatment program in Colorado, argued that the many kinesthetic learners are left behind by classical education. These young people learn best by stimulating sensory nerve endings in muscles, joints, and tendons. These students receive information best through touch and motion. Many youths exhibiting symptoms of hyperarousal receive information more easily through hands-on, kinesthetic programming. Helpful curricula include classes in shop, physical education, sewing and cooking, music, and fine arts. For hyperaroused youths experiencing extreme stress in their lives, the first educational step may be to help these young people feel secure, safe, and calm. Ironically, self-soothing is often achieved through motion and touch.

In his book, *Multiple Intelligences,* Gardner (1993) suggested seven intelligences: musical, bodily-kinesthetic, logical-mathematical, linguistic, spatial, interpersonal, and intrapersonal. He cited wonderful illustrations of these last two gifts—Anne Sullivan in her work with Helen Keller as an example of the possession of interpersonal intelligence, and the latter, Virginia Woolf.

Exposure to the trauma of child abuse may play a significant role in how and why academic achievement is developed in young people. A helpful study was conducted by Cynthia Perez and Cathy

Widom (1994). They interviewed almost 700 young adults with documented abuse histories (including neglect) before age eleven. They also interviewed members of a control group whom they matched for socioeconomic status, race, and age. They interviewed members of the experimental group approximately twenty years after the abuse had taken place. The interviewees and the interviewers were blind to the purpose of the study, which was to learn if there was a significant difference in reading ability and in IQ scores between the two groups. The participants in the study were given standardized reading and IQ tests and the results were startling. "More than 50% of the abused and/or neglected individuals as young adults have standard scores for reading ability (WRAT-R) in the deficient range . . . compared to less than 30% of the controls" (Perez and Widom, 1994, p. 623). In the same study, the researchers found, "Abused and neglected children completed significantly fewer years of school than control children . . . Indeed, 58% of the abused/neglected groups did not complete high school compared to 34% of the controls" (p. 625). IQ score differences were also noted. "The mean standard score for the controls is somewhat lower than national norms (90-99) and that for the abused and/or neglected individuals is about two standard deviations below the norm (mean standard score range 80-89)" (p. 623).

The issues concerning education are so entangled that separation of these issues is a tough challenge for child advocates. For instance, a young African-American youth who has been traumatized by terror and violence in the neighborhood may show symptoms of hyperarousal (e.g., poor concentration and agitation). That youth needs access to a myriad of resources. With respect to the youth's ethnic and racial background, McGeorge Bundy, who was president of the Ford Foundation, took the position, "There is no racially neutral process of choice that will produce more than a handful of minority students in our competitive colleges and professional schools" (Ravitch, 1983, p. 287). If the impact of racism is compounded with traumatic stress, the young person may need access to assistance in dealing with both issues.

In addition, some young persons in this country feel they must live for the moment, as if the future has been taken away. This may be an adaptive response to traumatic stress, a feeling of foreshortened sense of future. Tony, the young self-identified Skinhead discussed in Chapter 1, attended a public high school for a semester, earned straight As, and then quit. The challenge of getting As was just that, another life challenge. He was absorbed by the thrill of the demand. Once the demand was met, the excitement dissipated. The meaning of life for Tony and for some other young people is the intensity of staying alive. Ordinary aspects of living, such as holding a job, maintaining a consistent relationship with others, and earning a high school diploma are reduced to what it means to survive. Many youths are staying alive, but the price to themselves, to their families, and to society is grave. When Tony was asked to have faith in a meaning for life other than his own day-to-day challenges, his response was, "God can kiss my ass!"

The depth of anger, disappointment, and distrust that is often unleashed is primitive and animalistic. These young people need to be tamed before they will be ready to move beyond Maslow's (1968) first hierarchical tier of needs—food, shelter, and safety. There is an inherent desperation about a teenager engrossed in this basic struggle. Competent, specific, and creative educational programming must be made available for these adolescents—which is built on the establishment of morally solid, committed, nurturing relationships with teachers. Damon (1995) defined today's tragedy well: "Too many of today's teachers work with an air of professional detachment from their students, allowing students to just get by with minimal contributions and efforts" (p. 198); "All instruction flows from relationships" (p. 216).

Jonathan Kozol (1991) gave an unsettling description of a youngster's life:

> [He reflects on] a memory from 1965. An eight-year-old, a little boy who is an orphan, goes to the school to which I've been assigned. He talks to himself and mumbles during class but he is never offered psychiatric care or counseling. When he annoys his teacher, he is taken to the basement to be whipped. He isn't the only child in the class who seems to understand that he is being ruined, but he is the child who first captures my attention. His life is so hard and he is so small; and he is shy and still quite gentle. He has one gift: He draws

delightful childish pictures, but the art instructor say he "muddies his paints." She shreds his work in front of the class. Watching this, he stabs a pencil point into his hand.

Seven years later he is in the streets. He doesn't use drugs. He is an adolescent alcoholic. Two years later he has a child he can't support and he does not pretend to try. In front of Lord & Taylor he is seen in a long leather coat and leather hat. To affluent white shoppers he is the embodiment of evil. He laughs at people as they come out of the store; his laugh is like a pornographic sneer. Three years later I visit him in jail. His face is scarred and ugly. His skull is mapped with jagged lines where it was stitched together poorly after being shattered by a baseball bat. He does not at all resemble the shy child that I knew ten years before. He is regarded as a kind of monster now. He was jailed for murdering a white man in a wheelchair. I find him a lawyer. He is given 20 years.

To any retrospective pleas that I may make on his behalf, I hear a stock reply: How much exactly does a person have the right to ask? We did not leave this child in the street to die. We put him in a foster home. We did not deny him education. We assigned him to a school. Yes, you can tell us that the school was segregated, dirty, poorly funded, and the books were torn and antiquated, and the teachers unprepared. Nonetheless, it was a school. We didn't give him nothing. He got something. How much does a person have the right to ask? (pp. 194-195)

Kozol believed there is:

The lifelong deformation of poor children by their own society and government. . . . The manufacture of desire for commodities that children of low income can't afford also pushes them to underground economies and crime to find the money to appease the longings we have often fostered. Here, too, market forces are available to push them into further degradation. Gambling and prostitution have been centered now for many decades in inner city neighborhoods. Heroin sales to whites as well as blacks were centered in Boston's black South End and Roxbury as long [ago] as 1945. (p. 191)

Are not the youngsters who survive neighborhoods of such degradation real heroes and heroines? There are only small pockets of help for these young people—perhaps only eyedroppers full. In the Denver area, there are several antigang programs. There are counselors and residential programs that have sound reputations. However, unmet needs are visible throughout the city.

Poverty issues play a large role in the loss of hope of adolescents. Youths worry about their caretakers and whether or not their caretakers can make ends meet. Data from an early 1990s study compiled by the National Center for Education Statistics described the math scores of public school eighth graders in Iowa, North Dakota, and Minnesota as being as high as the scores of students in the high achieving countries of Korea and Taiwan. However, in the poorer states of Louisiana and Mississippi, the math scores of public school students looked more like those of Jordan, a developing country (Berliner and Biddle, 1995).

In a *Time* magazine article on the rap singer Ice-T, the reporter, Sally Donnelly (1992), quoted him as stating that, "It wasn't a cop or social worker who got me here . . . it was my boys, like the ones on death row, who are the reason I'm doing it" (p. 68). He is crediting the support of his peers as the reason for his success, not the support of a sparse human services network.

In the same article, an intriguing statement was made by Doug Elder, President of the Houston Police Officers Association. Elder voiced his disapproval of Ice-T's lyrics, with a warning about the explosiveness of mixing Ice-T's lyrics, violence, and drugs. It is hard to believe that so many people in this country do not understand that there currently exists a reign of terror for youngsters in many neighborhoods and families in this country. A testimony to the reality of it all can be found in many rap singers' lyrics, such as those in Ice-T's "New Jack Hustler": "Turned the needy into the greedy with cocaine . . . got me twisted . . . every dollar I get another brother drops" (Donnelly, 1992, p. 66).

Another interesting artist who literally capitalized on describing some of the worst of horrors that could be endured by few is Stephen King. He is an educator of sorts. He is able to take our minds and our hearts and painfully twist their reality base, an experience that traumatized youths endure in everyday life. With Stephen King there is no intellectual innocence. Even his titles characterize terror and fear: *The Dead Zone, The Shining, The Body, Pet Sematary, It.*

Moving away from Stephen King and terror and back to the sublime education of our youths, the following excerpt is from Jerome Bruner (1960). Notice how the assimilation and organization of information is so academically innocent. Notice how mind-boggling it is to juxtapose Bruner to King. This seems to be the task of our schools. Schools need to teach the full range of human thinking—from savage fantasy to academic scholarship.

> A tour of the United States in the summer of 1959 would have revealed a concentration of distinguished mathematicians in Boulder, Colorado, engaged in writing new textbooks for primary, junior high, and high school grades. In Kansas City, there could be found a group of first-class biologists busily producing films on subjects such as the structure of the cell and photosynthesis for use in tenth-grade biology courses. In Urbana, Illinois, there was a flurry of work on the teaching of fundamental mathematical concepts to a grade-school child, and in Palo Alto one might have found a mathematical logician at work trying out materials for teaching geometry to children in the beginning grades of school. (Bruner, 1960, pp. vii-viii)

Impoverished neighborhoods and language barriers are among the many other concerns that stir the anger of citizenry across the nation. Jonathan Kozol (1991), in his book *Savage Inequalities,* described the third world of East St. Louis, Illinois. Kozol described a litany of tragic life circumstances, such as the welfare population of the city (75 percent); high rates of homicides; a paucity of gynecological care, and high rates of fetal and infant deaths; a shortage of dental care; and many other examples of shortfalls besieging the citizens. One high school, East St. Louis High, is characterized as a disgrace to our country. Kozol portrayed this city's woeful high school system as having too few textbooks, too many substitute teachers, science labs without access to water, sports teams with nine year old uniforms, no goal posts on the football field, and other shortcomings.

The language problems in many cities seem to be less dramatic but nonetheless perplexing. In 1974, the Bilingual Education Act was passed, but the American Institutes for Research did not find promising results from the bilingual programs established under this act (Ravitch, 1983). English is a complicated language even for those who have grown up with its intricacies. Many immigrant children are not learning the language well. Too many American-born young people are not learning to speak other languages well. Some special education programs do not teach foreign languages at all.

CREATIVE THINKING

There must be a much clearer understanding of who is being educated. There must be the realization that education is for those who act beastly as well as those who act sublimely. The former act on the demands of the day just to survive. They have often been raised in ruthlessly cruel environments, have little or no vision for the future, and are forced into using all courageous and creative means at their disposal to survive. Their survival techniques will need to be matched by equally creative teachers and educational administrators.

Today, with the diversity of experience embodied in any one academic grade, it is paramount to offer students choices. The structure of educational space plays a very important role in creating a "holding environment" for youths. One example, for a large junior and senior high school population, is based on the model of "schools within a school." This model would be designed similarly to the college model. Students would have more choices—reducing the stigma attached to nonconformity. A large building would be divided architecturally into areas where small educational communities could work and grow together. To illustrate, one high school, or several in alliance, would offer: (1) an honors liberal arts school; (2) a traditional school; (3) an international school, specializing in diverse languages and cultures; (4) a specialized school helping youths overcome physical and perceptual difficulties; and (5) a school of the arts, for music, dance, and fine arts.

Flexibility should be emphasized so that a youth could take classes in several of the schools at one time, or spend a full semester in one of the schools—whatever would satisfy the youth's needs, educationally and otherwise. All students from the district would be included.

There is an actual model for "schools within schools": District 4, East Harlem, New York. This district serves approximately 3,500 junior high school students and has created over twenty separate programs which are staffed with minimal expense for administrative overhead (Toch, 1991).

A nonprofit, nonpartisan, national organization called Cities in Schools, developed in the 1980s, was devoted to providing more school-based services to struggling youths. By the early 1990s, there were many Cities in Schools throughout the United States. The services which this movement encouraged to be placed in schools included probation monitoring, child protection, and nursing. In some districts, retired citizens were recruited to come into the schools to share their wisdom. According to Dryfoos (1994) in his book, *Full-Service Schools*, when these schools housed well-trained professionals with reasonable workloads, wonderful opportunities for adequate support were offered to young people and their families.

Another model is the alternative school—usually housed separately from the larger mainstream public education buildings. An advantage to this model is that often young people who have endured traumatic life experiences identify with the creative aspects of alternative education. After all, these young people have already endured an "alternative life." A smaller building, housing fewer students and fewer bureaucrats, feels safer and more personalized. A disadvantage to this model is that usually the resources of these schools are very limited. Youths attending these innovative environments, often run by loving, dedicated teachers, do not have access to solid physical education departments, fine arts departments, and/or music departments. For example, Hampden Academy was formerly housed in the administrative building of a community mental health center. Not only did the students not have access to a playing field outside their door, but they often commented on how difficult it was to tell their friends where they attended school. More normalized settings are less stigmatizing to our young people.

An example of a primary school model would be a classical curriculum adapted in all classrooms to the different learning styles of the students. Each classroom would include the diversity of American children, and each classroom teacher would be competent in addressing diversity in physical, perceptual, and behavioral adaptations. A preventive strategy for teachers in primary grades would be to slow down the feedback loop and employ the tedium of rote and repetition to help youngsters learn the importance of sustained effort. Boredom is safe!

On the other hand, teenagers who have traumatic backgrounds often have an intense and immediate need for integrating stimuli, as demonstrated by their love for video games. These teenagers frequent convenience stores, malls, and arcades across the country, to play these games, and many youths own video games. Slowing down the feedback loop in junior and senior high school for these youths is tough. Once traumatized children move into adolescence, they would rather overthrow the classroom than tolerate a slowed-down approach to learning.

Schools enter into a relationship with our young people which spans approximately 15,000 hours, K-12. Educational institutions that address the needs of teenagers are in the toughest position. Secondary education is faced with teaching some children who are prepared for more generalized, abstract learning, and some who are not. Some youth's learning styles and learning abilities are more suited to the rigors of classical learning and others are not. Because classical skills are important to help young people share in the prosperity of this country, there is a national need to become more creative in teaching. The notions of community and full-service schools are beginning to give young people the message that adult professionals want to embrace whatever differences and difficulties young people may have.

The leadership skills needed by people in the various districts and schools across the United States—to structurally implement programs that include all teenagers—are great. Once philosophical arguments are brought into the arena of collaboration nationally in terms of public education in this country (again, this implies resolution of ambivalent attitudes), then the salient issue becomes an issue of design. How can schools be designed to meet the needs of teenagers and children?

There is a public elementary school, P. S. 121, in New York supported by the well-known philanthropist, Eugene Lang. In the 1980s, he provided college scholarship money and encouraged the development of supportive counseling and tutoring services to the students of this East Harlem school. He was told he would be lucky if only several of the P. S. 121 students made it through high school. In the early 1990s, six youths had earned college degrees, and over twenty-five others were attending college (Berliner and Biddle, 1995).

There are two schools in Colorado that stand out as models. One is P. S. 1, a new school in downtown Denver. From their charter application of November 1994, the Leadership Team stated, "P. S. 1's mission is to educate young people by enabling them to work as a learning community on challenging projects that enrich city life. In the process, they will be drawn toward higher and higher standards of character, conduct, work, academic achievement and community service."

The three-member Leadership Team collaborated in open, monthly council meetings with parents, youths, and community leaders for two years to establish this model school. Each student has a Personal Learning Plan (PLP) and an advisor. Classroom/workshop size is approximately one teacher to fifteen students. The size of the student body, grades five through nine, is around 125. Workshops are offered and open to all students. The workshops a student attends and when he or she will attend is part of the PLP. Examples of workshops offered are literature, writing, mathematics, and computer skills. Also, P. S. 1 offers opportunities for apprenticeships, internships, and for students to participate in city enhancement projects and other civic activities. P. S. 1 students are not structured by grade. The school is looking to the state for guidance in using special performance examinations based on state content standards rather than a test like the Iowa Test of Basic Skills, which evaluates uniformity in learning.

Lastly, the structure encourages a "hidden curriculum." This includes the architectural design of space, the quality of relationships, the degree of nurturing, the enthusiasm for learning, and the values cherished and practiced—all leading to the establishment of a community that can "hold" children and adolescents safely, lovingly, and inspirationally.

The other model school in Colorado is the splendidly named Eagle Rock School, a residential school snuggled into the cliffs of the Rocky Mountains outside of Estes Park, and it has a similar "hidden curriculum." This school is dedicated to teenagers ages fifteen to eighteen who have not had successful experiences in their home schools. Eagle Rock was created and financed by American Honda Corporation. During the early 1990s, Honda's corporate leaders made a decision to provide an outstanding service to America, and the recommendations came clearly to Honda to help educate the young. The school offers tuition-free education.

At Eagle Rock School, the architecture of the lab buildings, dorms, classroom buildings, development center, and teachers' homes creates the setting of a mountain village found in another land. Again, the leadership team and professional staff of this school are talented and dedicated to providing the best learning environment possible to their students. At the ends of trimesters, students are guided by their teachers to give "Presentations of Learning." These presentations can vary from describing a complicated physics project to demonstrating proficiency in a foreign language. The presentations are both informative and inspirational to other students and teachers— strengthening the growth of the students and the community.

In the United States, as we enter the twenty-first century, the plight of many adolescents can be addressed in the schools by an educational curriculum that focuses on recognizing and preserving human rights. The concept of traumatic stress can be linked to the violations or betrayals of civil rights and integrated in social studies curricula. An educational curriculum that addresses civil rights violations worldwide would help teenagers who have been traumatized by child abuse to develop a framework for moral development.

Thinking

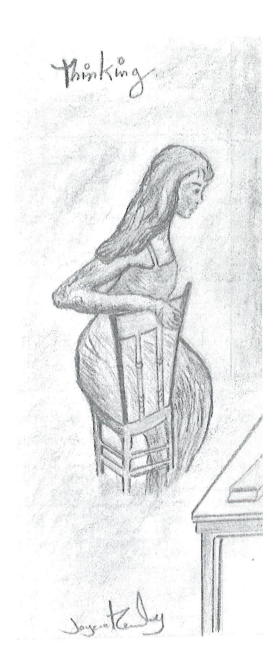

Joyce Kewley

Chapter 6

Mental Health

Mental health is the last system to be discussed. Community mental health centers, private and public psychiatric hospitals, therapeutic group homes, day treatment programs, private practitioners, and various continua of care comprise this system. While diagnostic categories are designed to help illuminate the clinical presentation of individuals, they often serve to focus on symptoms to the exclusion of the whole person. The following examples, contained in the records of adolescents discharged from hospitals and entering less restrictive treatment settings in a large metropolitan area in the 1990s, illustrate the overpathologizing of symptoms of trauma that can be associated with diagnostic labels from the *Diagnostic and Statistical Manual of Mental Disorders* (American Psychiatric Association, 1994):

- A fifteen-year-old boy who had been sexually assaulted and physically abused was diagnosed as follows: Axis I: Undifferentiated conduct disorder; Axis II: Personality disorder, NOS (not otherwise specified), with impulsive, schizoid, delinquent dynamic features.
- A fourteen-year-old boy was given the following diagnoses: Axis I: Conduct disorder, solitary aggressive; major depression, recurrent; Axis II: Borderline personality disorder; identity disorder. This boy had been abandoned by his father and moved to and from three foster homes in a six-month period.
- A fifteen-year-old girl was described with the following clinical picture: Axis I: Depressive disorder, NOS; polysubstance abuse; Axis II: Personality disorder with narcissistic features. She had witnessed frequent and ongoing brutal beatings of her mother and was herself sexually assaulted.

These labels do not explain the context of the lives of these young people. The labels too often merely serve to conveniently classify youths into readily available categories that take the young people out of the context of their lives with behavioral interventions, such as incarceration.

What are the implications for helping youths who have these labels? First, the labels are overwhelming for therapists, educators, and the individuals themselves. Imagine how teenagers feel when they actually discover what they have been labeled. Secondly, these psychiatric labels tend to be misleading and sometimes inaccurate. A personality disorder diagnosis suggests a pervasive pattern that is not easily altered. Repeatedly, clinicians have experienced youths with these diagnoses changing their patterns of behavior. As for the issues of identity fluctuations and narcissism, they are associated with important normal struggles of adolescence and thus are not accurately categorized as illnesses. Most important, these labels neglect to account for the etiology of the struggles of many youths in general.

The "dignity factor" in the recovery process is just beginning to be appreciated by mental health professionals. The courageous disclosure in 1991 by Marilyn Van Derbur Atler, formerly Miss America 1958 from Colorado, of her father perpetrating incest against her during childhood and adolescence, has helped to open the eyes of the public to the suffering from sexual assault. This woman suffered the pain and indignity of that trauma for nearly forty years. After revealing the wrenching experience, she became an ambassador for the cause of child abuse prevention. Mrs. Atler captivated an audience of professionals at a luncheon during the Ninth Annual Child Abuse Conference in Denver in September 1991, stating that she was introduced at the Miss America Pageant just months before as an incest survivor. For the first time she said she "had no shame." She was on her way to recovery. Certainly there are many other people who have courageously taken this path to recovery as well.

It is important to mention at this time that not all young people traumatized by child abuse act out to the degree described by many of the youths in this book. Marilyn Van Derbur Atler showed scholarship throughout her academic career and lived an externally exemplary life. Growing up, she was numbed by her trauma until she was ready to let go of her own creative adaptation to it. However, during her disclosure she also revealed that some early attempts at recovery with professional help were unhelpful. The fact that so many teenagers have not had their mental health needs met is a perplexing and tragic public health issue. In unraveling the complexities, teenagers and adults are often working against themselves and each other.

Teenagers are not always truthful, as traumatized youth often present a facade of their fragile selves. In the classic book by John Knowles, *A Separate Peace* (1959), the narrator, Gene Forrester, used the personality of his best friend, Phineas, to camouflage his anger and deceit. Phineas, by contrast, takes chances and expresses feelings honestly, letting Gene in on the secret that he, Gene, is his best friend. "Finny" tells Gene, "I hope you're having a pretty good time here. I know I kind of dragged you away at the point of a gun, but after all, you can't come . . . by yourself, and at this teenage period in life the proper person is your best pal" (p. 55). Gene is incapable of dealing with Finny's honesty. He is too phony. He lives in the shadow of his best friend. Or as he speaks of himself, ". . . I lost part of myself to him . . . , and a soaring sense of freedom revealed that this must have been my purpose from the first: to become a part of Phineas" (p. 103). Another example of this lack of identity was when Gene sneaked into the infirmary where Phineas was sick and not to be disturbed. Gene said, "I thought I belonged here" (p. 236).

Toward the end of the novel, Gene reflects upon his own superficial existence:

> My whole life at Devon has been a dream, or rather that everything at Devon, the playing fields, the gym, the water hole, and all the other buildings and all the people there were intensely real, wildly alive and totally meaningful, and I alone was a dream, a figment which had never really touched anything. (pp. 232-233)

Gene Forrester was an angry student. His friend, Leper, referred to him as uncivilized, telling him, "[You] always were a savage underneath" (p. 180).

During a time when Gene and Phineas were getting along well, Gene said, "I wanted to break out crying from the stabs of hopeless joy, or intolerable promise, or because these mornings were too full of beauty for me, because I knew of too much hate to be contained in a world like this" (p. 65). After Phineas's death, Gene said, "My fury was gone. I felt it gone, dried up at the source, withered and lifeless" (p. 255).

Sometimes mental health professionals have worked against the comprehensive needs of adolescents. This has occurred within the context of historical threads influencing the education of mental health workers. In other words, the needs of a given individual or family often must fit into the treatment of a given clinician. Needless to say, all clients do not have the same needs. Family therapy, for example, might be helpful to some families, but destructive to others. Clinicians need to be cautious not to fit youths and families into treatment assumptions. Thorough initial and ongoing assessments are essential in the treatment of any client population.

A thorough assessment of such a young person would include a mental status examination, psychosocial history, assessment of cultural factors (such as ethnicity, race, gender, sexual orientation, spiritual beliefs, socioeconomic level), family and peer relationships, assessment of need for a medical evaluation, precipitating factors, coping mechanisms, developmental issues, and history of trauma. No assessment should be based solely on behavior. With a thorough assessment, a variety of clinical issues can be ruled in or out. For example, a teenager who is currently being abused in his home would run away for very different reasons than a young person who had a significant substance abuse problem.

Randy's Story

Randy, a fourteen-year-old who had run away from home three times (one time hitchhiking a ride out of state, and another time taking off overnight on his skateboard), was taken to a managed care facility by his parents for a psychiatric evaluation. From his early childhood, he had had a history of horrendous physical abuse that required extensive medical treatment. Parental rights were terminated. He was subsequently adopted by his current family. Randy's family members told their story to an intake worker who assigned the family to a therapist with a structural family therapy background. For one year, the entire family faithfully participated in family therapy. Each of the members was assigned tasks, such as dad not disciplining the boy for a week while allowing the mother to set limits and be responsible for the primary parenting. Another intervention included one of the members of the family participating in individual growth-oriented treatment.

Randy's run behavior subsided for awhile and then started up again. Finally, one night he was found by the police, dressed in a disheveled way, without shoes, sitting under a bridge. He was acutely psychotic. His parents were mortified. He has been hospitalized psychiatrically several times since then. It seems that the issues of trauma may have been overlooked.

HISTORICAL THREADS

Early themes in mental health history can hopefully shed light on the need to integrate both professional education and agency intervention into coherent protocols to assess and treat teenagers. Historically, the conceptualization and treatment of traumatic stress was designed to help adults. There is a critical need for training of mental health workers in identifying and treating traumatic stress in children and adolescents.

There are two historical threads in viewing psychological trauma. First, from World War II came the phrase "traumatic war neurosis." The experience of war has been historically connected to the concepts of both physical and psychological trauma. From Holocaust survivors and Vietnam War veterans, we have learned about the profound effects of psychological trauma—more popularly called post-traumatic stress disorder. The movie *Born on the Fourth of July* (1989) portrays the tragic human cost of war. This terror from violence is powerfully described by Joseph Conrad ([1902] 1984) in his story, *Heart of Darkness*. The following quote is from a young man who travels by steamer into the jungle where violence is pervasive, but, symbolically, so much cannot be seen because of the density of the brush. Conrad wrote:

> I was completely unnerved by the sheer blank fright, pure abstract terror. . . . What made this emotion so overpowering was—how shall I define it?—the moral shock I received, as if

something altogether monstrous, intolerable to thought and odi-
ous to the soul, had been thrust upon me unexpectedly. (p. 141)

Today, violence in communities still shocks young people on
many levels.

The second historical thread has evolved from Freudian theory.
Dr. Henry Krystal (1978) in his paper "Trauma and Affects"
asserted that, "Freud's earliest and essential observation about psychic trauma, which remains the cornerstone of our understanding of
it, . . . [confirms] that some hysterical attacks are the aftereffects of
unbearable experiences in the past" (p. 82). Freud felt that people
who had experienced traumatic events were compelled to "repeat the
repressed material as a contemporary experience instead of remem-
bering it as something belonging to the past" (van der Kolk, 1991).

In the meantime, at the Paris hospital, Salpêtrière, Pierre Janet
was formulating an important theory based on the effects of trauma
on the human psyche. This theory, acknowledged in a paper by van
der Kolk and van der Hart (1989), found that "In hysteria the
primary mode of adaptation is the dissociation of feelings or memories related to frightening experiences, which results in a narrowing
of consciousness" (p. 1531). Janet recognized that significant
events in a patient's past caused what he referred to as "vehement
emotion." A patient who was unable to master the traumatic event
struggled with excessive reactions to other stresses (van der Kolk
and van der Hart, 1989). Janet urged that when treating individuals
by traumatic memory, "The individuals are brought to ruin because
they maintain a certain expenditure outside the channels of their
ordinary life and this hidden expense is too considerable for their
resources" (Janet, 1924, p. 272). Janet was referring to adult adaptation. Children and teenagers have fewer psychological resources to
bring to the child abuse "war zone."

The treatment of the ravages of child abuse was left to fall later
upon the community mental heath system. This system was created
in the 1960s under the Kennedy administration. However, the bible
of diagnosis and treatment in community mental health is the *Diagnostic and Statistical Manual of Mental Disorders* (American Psychiatric Association, 1994). It was not until 1994 that the effects of
child abuse were mentioned as categories of clinical attention in this

manual. Trauma theory as part of the development of the medical, psychodynamic model of assessment and treatment was not identified diagnostically in the first half of this century. It took the horrific suffering of war vets to rekindle the idea that traumatic life experiences, such as child abuse, impact mental health. Post-traumatic stress disorder was a diagnosis first defined in 1980.

The first mental health clinic, called a psychological clinic, was started one hundred years ago in Pennsylvania, under the auspices of the University of Pennsylvania, by Lightner Witmer. The inspiration for the clinic came from the paucity of help provided to poor school children. Witmer's clinic was the beginning of an integration of the comprehensive needs of young people. Witmer, who broadly educated himself in law, philosophy, and psychology, wanted comprehensive services for children. "He wanted to institute special or upgraded training classes for children who were mentally or physically disabled" (Levine and Levine, 1992, p. 33). He started a hospital school, and he wanted his clinic to be an educational resource for teachers. His theories included that of a diagnostic education. Therapeutic trainers would make assessments after they tried to teach something to a young person. Levine and Levine (1992) cited examples of Witmer's unwavering dedication to successfully educating the seemingly most disabled children.

It was also over one hundred years ago that William James ([1890] 1983) wrote his landmark book, *The Principles of Psychology*. James was intellectually sophisticated, holding a professorship at Harvard University, and he was individualistically driven. The scope of his work, although it certainly would address the mental life of an adolescent, neglected to integrate ecological factors. (Levine and Levine, 1992).

The settlement house movement at the turn of the century was designed to address ecological/social factors. Hull House in Chicago, founded by Jane Addams, took a social, ecological approach toward housing, food, and clothing issues; and providing nursing care, morally supportive services, and reading lessons (Levine and Levine, 1992). This movement seemingly neglected helping those individuals with major mental illness. Before the turn of the century, Dorothea Dix, appalled by the conditions in the correctional system, sought more humane hospital care for those with major mental illnesses. Today, adolescents are again faced with diminished hospital care and increased correctional interventions, often not providing mental health care.

At the end of World War I, the child guidance clinic gained momentum. A philanthropic organization called the Commonwealth Fund established a demonstration clinic to help public welfare. The Fund administrators collaborated with Clifford Beers, founder of the National Committee for Mental Hygiene, to focus on preventing delinquency. This initiative prompted staffings and open case conferences focusing on young people (Levine and Levine, 1992). This effort also led the way for family participation and the increasing popularity of family therapy techniques. However, although agency personnel were coming together, their orientations remained entrenched and cross-training was rare. In addition, parents were often seen as clients rather than partners in the acquisition of mental health, whether it was sought for themselves or for their children or both. Nevertheless, with the prevention of delinquency in mind, the emphasis was on having a team of professionals ". . . make an accurate medical, social and psychological diagnosis and transmit these scientific findings to personnel in the agency that referred the child" (Levine and Levine, 1992, p. 150).

This initiative of the Commonwealth Fund sounds very similar to initiatives in the United States in the 1990s, and what happened is also familiar. The comprehensive assessments were made by a team of professionals and then turned over to other agencies to implement. Other agencies were not adept at working together, and collaborative efforts were often ineffective. Needed institutional reform did not occur and a "shift in viewpoint prestaged an even greater emphasis on treatment centered on the confines of a therapy room, the consequent isolation of the clinics from other agencies" (Levine and Levine, 1992, p. 151).

In the 1960s, community mental health centers were created across the United States. And, as the community mental health centers gained momentum, the inpatient census in hospitals decreased. For children and adolescents, hospitalization can be both a blessing and a trauma. For youth at risk, the hospital provides wonderful safety and security. For youth dramatically victimizing themselves, hospitalization can extend dependency beyond reasonable limits.

Today, with the advent of managed health care and block-granted Medicaid dollars, company executives are looking to cut hospital costs and at the same time reframe the already inconsistently defined protocols of diagnosis and treatment. Alternatives to hospitalization may actually be more helpful to youths who are not imminently dangerous to themselves or others due to mental illness. Such programs for high-risk youths tend to be time-limited or have long waiting lists. They often do not meet the needs of young people who are essentially being raised in institutions. The development of programs for youths who have long histories of traumatization would fulfill a great need. In medical treatment, a diabetic patient is not put into a short-term model of taking insulin. If a diabetic person goes into insulin shock, hopefully hospital benefits are not used up.

One of the latest developments experienced in mental health is diagnosing at-risk youths with conduct disorders. This diagnosis is deemed the harbinger of an antisocial personality disorder and mostly thought of as untreatable, again leaving many children behind. Such a diagnosis looks at behavior, not etiology. The whole person is not viewed within the context of his or her life. Implying that a young person is untreatable seems destructive, and may eventually set up a self-fulfilling prophecy. These youths are often warehoused in correctional facilities, the very same political issue that Dorothea Dix fought against over one hundred years ago. Unfortunately, youths diagnosed with only a conduct disorder or with both a conduct disorder, particularly childhood-onset, and with PTSD, may inflict or re-enact harm to the community and to the people close to them.

Clinicians employed by community mental health centers are asked to address all kinds of problem areas ranging from depression to psychosis, from learning disabilities to delinquency, and from child abuse to murder, and they are asked to treat the myriad problems with narrowly focused educational backgrounds, often without important cross-training or access to interdisciplinary consultation. Clinicians are most often asked to tackle these ills in a "small cubicle."

The needs of an acting-out, traumatized adolescent certainly are not captured in a singular focus. It is unfortunate that the issues adults are grappling with today look so similar to the ones Levine and Levine (1992) described in the 1920s "The choice to work with the individual, in contrast with an attempt to work with the larger social structure is puzzling in the light of the virtual impossibility of meeting the immense demand for service by means of individual treatment" (p. 155).

Trauma has an impact on mental health in broad, profound ways. People can move on from traumatic stress, but meanings can be altered forever. The horrible tragedy of the bombing of the Alfred P. Murrah Federal Building in Oklahoma City on April 19, 1995, changed the lives of thousands of people. One hundred sixty-eight people were killed; children lost parents, brothers, and sisters; adults lost children, partners, and friends. Humane treatment protocols appropriate for beginning to meet the needs of the Oklahoma City survivors are being taught to university doctors, private practitioners, mental health professionals, and Red Cross personnel by the survivors themselves. Two years later, during the trial of Timothy McVeigh in Denver, a safe environment was created, providing a refuge for survivors. Mental health counselors, clergy, and other volunteers took special training to better understand the impact of trauma. Professionals were available to survivors on rotating shifts to listen to their stories and provide comfort. The refuge was a secure, safe place for survivors to meet. Youths who have felt the impact of the trauma of child abuse need this kind of comprehensive help by trained professionals.

CREATIVE LIVES

The following family story provides a further source of education for mental health professionals. This story is very important to the understanding of the generational nature of psychological trauma, in other words, how untreated or unresolved residue from trauma passes on to progeny.

Rachael and Susan's Stories

Rachael, a bright attractive young girl, entered an intensive therapy program for depression. The therapeutic team working with her was unable to help and she was eventually hospitalized for being a high suicide risk. Although she was much loved by her single-parent mother, she was unable to feel the love. This phenomenon is seen often in treating families with traumatic pasts. Because her mother, Susan, did not receive appropriate help, Rachael was left feeling abandoned by her mother. The pain from the traumatic experiences of both of their early childhoods was left unaddressed.

After the initial hospitalization, lasting several weeks, Rachael was settled into a residential child care facility. She was twelve years old. For the next four years she lived not only in the child care facility, but she was hospitalized eleven more times and placed in foster care. In 1992, her mother, having begun her own recovery, wrote the following beautiful poem. Soon after this poem was written, Rachael returned home.

> I do not have to run anymore.
> I do not have to scream to make my pain real and to let my children and me feel,
> I can feel without losing control.
> I can feel sleepy without tearing myself apart.
> I can stay whole without denying my children's pain, without telling them to "shut up."
> I can use my power without denying my children's need to cry, even to whine.
> I can develop strength, but it doesn't have to be at the children's expense or to shut them down.
> I can be a dangerous "warrioress" too, but still honor and not terrorize my children. Someday maybe I'll set the limits of my feelings better.
> I can build a monument of internal strength that won't let me down and that my children can share at their level of participation. God gives it to me. I don't need a man; especially not a weak, taking man. Yet, I have love to give.
> It's hard to decide or know how much to give and when to step back and stop. How much is in my power range? What diminishes me as a powerful being?

The very saddest aspect of the recovery of this family was that while Rachael was placed out of the home, her mother maintained minimal contact with her. This loss, compounded with other losses, had a devastating impact on Rachael's will to live. In fact, her therapist believed the repeated hospitalizations were desperate attempts to reunite with the nurturing her mother had provided for her in early childhood. But the hospital did not represent safety to her mother. Every time Rachael entered another hospital, Susan felt more and more inadequate as a mother. The only way she knew how to modulate her feelings of failure was to stay away from her daughter. For many years, Rachael's mother did not understand her own struggle to overcome a traumatic past. Those around her did not understand either. Much of her current recovery she mastered on her own.

Susan knew no models in raising her children. She struggled to protect herself and her family from harm. Her oppressive childhood in Berlin after World War II taught her a present-oriented existence—an existence of getting through the suffering as well as she could. Her goodness was always visible. She had profound love for her children and contributed to others by volunteering on a rape crisis hot line.

The full degree of traumatic stress in Susan's past can be illuminated by Cornelius Ryan's (1966) book, *The Last Battle*. Ryan described Berlin in 1945: "Almost half of Berlin's 1,562,000 dwellings had sustained some kind of damage, and every third house was either completely destroyed or uninhabitable" (pp. 15-16). For women in particular, Berlin became a city of dread. "The fear of sexual attack lay over the city like a pall, for Berlin, after nearly six years of war, was now primarily a city of women" (p. 26). Even at a convent, Ryan described a priest as feeling inadequate to offer protection as he told sixty nuns and lay sisters that they needed to fear being raped (p. 26):

In the same convent,

> The resolute Mother Superior hoped the fighting would not be prolonged. What with an allied plane crashing in her orchard and the roof of her convent being blown off a few days before, the danger was coming much too close . . . She had more than two hundred people to care for: 107 newborn babies (of whom 91 were illegitimate), 32 mothers, and 60 nuns and lay sisters. (pp. 370-371)

"The merciless shelling had no pattern. It was aimless and incessant. Each day it seemed to increase in intensity" (p. 420). In one part of Berlin, "Homeless Germans were everywhere—along the roads, in the fields, villages and forests, sleeping in wagons, tents, broken-down trucks, railway carriages, and in the open" (p. 443).

The unending stories were horrific. One doctor working in a hospital "was appalled by the number of refugees who had attempted suicide—including scores of women who had not been molested or violated. Terrified by what they had witnessed or heard, many had slashed their wrists. Some had even tried to kill their children" (p. 31).

The degree of sexual exploitation of women described by Ryan is beyond comprehension. A woman "was raped at gunpoint before the eyes of her helpless husband and fifteen-year-old son; as soon as the Russians had left, the half-crazed husband shot his wife, his son and himself to death" (p. 491). Another woman,

> . . . A mother of three children had been dragged from her family and raped through an entire night. In the morning the woman was released; she rushed back to her youngsters—only to find her own mother and brother had hanged all three children and then themselves. The woman thereupon slashed her wrists and died. (p. 491)

This was the context for the beginning of Susan's life. Susan had been conceived by rape several years after Berlin fell.

PART III:
HEALING A GENERATION

All of the therapeutic techniques in the world will not be effective with a traumatized youth, or likely anyone else for that matter, unless a therapeutic relationship can be formed. Young people who have been abused, neglected, or otherwise mistreated by adults are keenly sensitized to the affect, attitudes, and sensitivity of others in their world. Whenever anxiety is heightened, such as during a first appointment with a new therapist, the level of attunement may be even greater.

Behold

Chapter 7

The Therapeutic Process

It is important to emphasize that a mental health clinician is not the only person whose relationship with a traumatized young person can make a difference. Healing relationships can take place between any two people. Paraprofessionals and volunteers, teachers or support staff in a school, neighbors, and other safe members of a community can provide the context for powerful healing to occur. In fact, assisting a young person in developing a healing community, rather than just an individual relationship, will allow the healing to expand exponentially.

The CASTT (Child Abuse Specific Treatment of Trauma) model, which will be explicated in Chapter 8, was based on the premise that authentic, caring relationships with traumatized youths are essential to recovery. This is even more true for those who have been chronically abused or neglected, or are struggling with additional burdens such as poverty, racism, and violence in their communities. These young people are not always initially appealing. Some may intimidate, dehumanize, or completely tune out adults who are attempting to make a connection with them. Previous connections with some—if not most—adults have been dangerous, disappointing, or ineffectual. It is in the best interests of self-preservation for traumatized youths to hesitate at connection again. It is the responsibility of the adults involved in making the connection to withstand the barrage of negativity or indifference directed at them by the adolescents. This testing is an inherent part of the process for young people who have suffered multiple rejections. Adult passage of such tests is an initial building block to create a bridge between the world of the helper and the island of the harmed.

The concept of authenticity, from self-in-relation theory (Jordan, Surrey, and Kaplan, 1982), was drawn on in the development of the CASTT model. A person in a therapeutic or healing role with an adolescent shares his or her identity. This sharing represents a powerful corrective for young people who have experienced abuse. The sharing does not necessarily involve personal disclosure on the part of the clinician, but it does represent an authentic connectedness on a human level. Therapists will likely have flexible roles with the adolescents, and with aspects of parenting, counseling, playing, and coaching.

The clinical role presents the most conflicts. It is artificial to maintain the same kinds of boundaries with youths that therapists maintain with adults. Successful adolescent trauma therapists do not want their clients or patients to feel like clients or patients unless there is a safety issue. They want their clients to feel like vibrant teenagers. Their relationship with a traumatized adolescent is not static. Sometimes the relationship feels good and other times it feels frustrating and discouraging. These are feelings often stirred through efforts to be good adult role models. These are real feelings in an authentic relationship with an adolescent.

If a youth presents high-risk behavior and there are imminent safety concerns, the mental health professional must prioritize the safety of the young person and the community. Even though youths discuss scary, dangerous plans in efforts to manipulate responses, when they present as suicidal or homicidal, teenagers need to be placed in a safe, supervised setting for further evaluation. In developing an authentic relationship, a therapist needs to integrate his or her professional and personal self. The professional stance is clearly stated at the beginning of the therapeutic relationship with a young person through the ten-point framework describing goals for adolescent recovery from traumatic stress. The therapist recognizes traumata in young people's lives up front through a history gathering process, while letting each one know that his or her journey will be unique and that many youths have made remarkable recoveries from hardship.

The therapist lets a young person know through words that he or she loves working with adolescents, and that he or she is concerned about the suffering the teenager has endured, the violations of civil rights, and the possible ensuing moral degradation.

Mostly, experienced therapists encourage traumatized young people to feel empowered, and try not to strip away an ounce of their self-reliance and social responsibility. A therapist needs to be determined to meet these teenagers on as much of an equal footing as the therapist can endure, even if they are behaving and thinking outrageously. Therefore, right at the start of therapy, the therapist expects the youths to keep up with the therapist's challenges. The therapist listens only briefly to war stories, and challenges the decisions of teenagers to remain victims.

If a youth interrupts the clinician, uses poor English, or manifests distorted thinking, the therapist will provide instructional responses. In return, if therapists are missing the whole point, these young people do correct them. In essence, throughout the sessions, skilled therapists often tell teenagers about the hopes and expectations they have for them. This authentic style of relating to a traumatized teenager earns the respect of the adolescent more easily. It also shows that the therapist understands the broad range of guidance these youths often need.

Adolescent trauma therapists behave in an adult-directed manner, a style that breaks away from overt active listening. This style employs the philosophy of listening with a "Third Ear," as Theodor Reik (1949, p. 159) called this form of hearing. It is listening to what a youth will not say—listening to silence. Empathy is always preserved.

A method for helping a therapist to listen with a "Third Ear" is for the therapist to use the technique of thinking aloud to himself or herself, as if pondering a question of self-interest, in an attempt to draw a youth into a discussion that focuses on real issues. For instance, a therapist might comment, "It seems to me that young people today are expected to grow up in an unprincipled world." Then the therapist might name the principles that are important for young people to be exposed to and to emulate: respect, honesty, moderation, even temperament, courage, self-discipline, sustained effort, friendship. The therapist then askd the adolescent, "What do you think about the principles I just named?" As mentioned previously, traumatized adolescents wear masks and often do not speak the truth, so the teenager may respond with a grunt or a retort such as, "Dream on." This is just what an experienced adolescent therapist expects and is now ready to challenge the teenager's position. "I wonder what your life would be like if you followed these principles? Just imagine sustained effort in English class!" After bantering for quite some time, the therapist can let the young person know that he or she believes the youth could earn an A in English with sustained effort. This bantering must be followed up experientially. The therapist might then review a student's English paper.

Often, with children who have been traumatized, cortical messages are not received. The part of the brain that would receive them is not turned on. Repetition and experience help to change the brain (Perry, 1996). For example, Carlee, mentioned in Chapter 2, learned sustained effort through hours and hours of practicing the piano. The following stories are two more examples to illustrate these points further:

Joanne's Story:

Joanne was applying to graduate schools, but was limiting her choices to schools within her midwestern home state. Her mother empathically listened while Joanne reviewed her choices. There also happened to be two excellent graduate schools on the East coast representing her field of study. Her mother asked her if she had considered either of them. Joanne responded, "No! Those schools are too hard." Up to this time, her mother had been supportive as both a parent and as an active listener, but changing her demeanor, she blurted out, "I think you have not thought through the issue carefully. I think your decision is driven by the fear of not being accepted at the schools in the East. Making a decision based on fear will not be a sound decision. I think most definitely you need to apply to the two Eastern schools." Joanne did apply to both schools, and ultimately graduated from one of them. She has since told her mother that had her mother not been so insistent, she would not have applied.

Another young woman did not, unfortunately, have such an invested counselor or mother:

Linda's Story:

Shortly before Linda graduated in the top of her class from high school, she was faced with the traumatic death of her father. Her bereaved mother did not feel she could manage the financial responsibilities of the family. She solicited help from her daughter. Linda did not know whether to go on to college or work, so she went to a school counselor for help. The school counselor listened empathically to the agonizing conflict of the young woman, but he offered no direct help. Basically, he identified the dimensions of the conflict and told Linda that she was capable of making a good decision for herself. She finally made the decision to work and help her mother. Later in her adulthood, Linda stated that what she had needed from her high school counselor was to be told that she was one of the brightest students in the school and that she could get a scholarship to most any college she chose. She needed to be told that the counselor cared about her future and that he would help arrange support for her mother. The biggest regret of Linda's life was not going on to college from high school.

Many youths need directive therapeutic help or help in healing, but in no direct way are they going to ask for it. In particular, youths traumatized by child abuse do not, in most instances, want therapy. They say that they do not want another person in their lives. A skilled adolescent therapist presents himself or herself authentically and with self-confidence to a traumatized adolescent while validating the young person's disgust with the thought of receiving therapy. This is the first step in the therapeutic process. The second undertaking is to attract them to the guide rope—the therapist. Therapists need to decide what part of themselves to give.

Humor, if used appropriately, can be a wonderful tool with teenagers and their families. Having cartoons with themes relevant to the lives of teenagers, such as sloppy rooms, the "couch potato" syndrome, school issues, and instant meals can be used as tools for connecting. In addition, a selection of wigs can be used in working with parents who reprimand their children for small matters, such as sloppy rooms. Lending a wig to parents with the direction that they wear it when their son or daughter's room looks terrible, and keep it on until the room looks better—even if it means going to the store wearing the wig, can sometimes deescalate an otherwise difficult situation.

The mission of the therapist is to function like a guide rope that lifts young people derailed by life experiences back onto a healthy track. The definition of the track, the length of the rope, and the recovery time are reached through a collaborative therapeutic or recovery process. The youth is always in control and is able to throw aside the guide rope at any time.

The role of the therapist is complex. The needs of these adolescents are complex. Traditional therapy models do not appear to be consistently effective. The degree of skill of the therapist does not seem to be a factor either. The ineffectiveness of the mental health system in general in treating severely traumatized youths may have to do with not having defined the breadth of the struggle of these youths more accurately. Fortunately, traumatized teenagers respond to a loving, authentic relationship and environment.

Multiexpression relationships may be very helpful in working with these young people. The five ways through which a therapist might express himself or herself to traumatized teenagers are love, play, work, teaching, and parenting. Any one or more of these expressions may come out during a therapy session. Going back to the guide rope metaphor, the rule is not to pull too hard unless the place where a young person may be hanging is precarious. Then giving a quick tug often works.

Letting the youth know you think he or she is terrific, or letting a young person know that you believe in him or her are acts of love. Other examples would include calling a youth when you know he or she has just taken a tough exam, or taking the youth out to breakfast. Emphasizing the guide rope metaphor, loving is like gently tugging or encouraging a young person to move forward. Loving a young person is letting the teenager know she or he is important to you.

Play can take the form of unending wonderful experiences with teenagers, such as organized and spontaneous games, water pistol and food fights, play with makeup—the list goes on and on. Playing is shaking the guide rope; teenagers adore risk and adventure.

Teaching is an important facet of helping traumatized teenagers. Reviewing academic subjects to build self-confidence or just simply teaching the dimensions of normal responses of adolescents to trauma can be helpful. Another helpful area of teaching is ethics. Moral development has become complicated as we move into the twenty-first century. Teenagers are not as apt to follow convention. Their moral development must shift sharply from not misbehaving due to punishment to not misbehaving due to some higher meaning, like not wanting to do harm. If the teenagers themselves have been harmed, one can understand how difficult moral learning is. Teaching values and presenting them in an historical sense—addressing the outcomes of various value choices, such as sexual promiscuity increasing the odds of contracting AIDS—is an essential element in helping young people traumatized by child abuse.

The last dimension of help that these young people often need is coparenting. Specific ways to demonstrate parental caring to these young people are by: keeping them safe, worrying about them, arguing with them, crying with them, and being a cheerleader for them. Showing a depth of concern to people who have been uncared for can be deeply therapeutic. If teenagers have great parents or other caretakers, a therapist can team up with the caretakers. No young person can have too many people caring for his or her well being.

Therapists will likely get lost for short periods of time. Traumatized youths are creative self-healers. Metaphorically, this is the time to allow the youth to let go of the rope. But these times must not discount those when a youth has a firm grip on the rope. Therapists need to maintain their connections especially during such times. The rope remains ready to be picked up at any time during treatment.

The strength of the rope or therapist, in pulling a young person on to a healthy track, is vital. Youths derailed by child abuse must change the traditions and rituals in their lives. They are without a proud heritage. Changing a heritage is a tremendous challenge to adults; to teenagers the changes often seem impossible. Therapists must give the parts of themselves needed to complement the weaknesses of youths. Helping them compensate and fortify themselves for the necessary work ahead is essential. Giving teenagers tennis lessons during "therapy sessions" or skiing with them can be used as wonderful forms of metaphoric communication—such as mastering a top-spin forehand or a mogul run. Without change, teenagers risk losing their entire childhoods to combating traumatic stress.

Appropriate self-disclosures and the shedding of personal disguises also add to the development of an authentic relationship. If a therapist and youth can establish this depth of relationship, the therapist will have the privilege of watching a young person begin to realize his or her own real power and use it to change and grow. Failing at establishing a real relationship with a young person will likely lead to a failure to be helpful.

The final mission of an adolescent trauma therapist (traditionally called the termination process), is to move the rope away, and see the traumatized youth stand strong on his or her own successful track.

It is important to be reminded of Dr. van der Kolk's words, "Traumatized people are more dissimilar than similar" (personal communication, 1991). Each youth's journey is different. Forming real, individualized connections will facilitate the process of healing.

Therapists working with traumatized youths need to assess their own value systems, as these will likely be conveyed unconsciously to clients. Helpful values include commitment to social justice, respect for client rights and life choices, and appreciation of diversity. Understanding human behavior on an individual and social level is also of use. The vast social systems within which a given person lives have an incredible impact on development. In other words, biology and family history are as important as social factors such as race, ethnicity, gender, sexual orientation, and socioeconomic background.

RESPONSIBILITIES OF A THERAPIST TREATING ADOLESCENTS

The leadership demands on a therapist who treats adolescents are labor intensive. A therapist provides a healing environment for a youth who has been harmed. The word therapy is derived from the Greek word *therapia*, to provide a service or to act as an attendant. John Briere (1989) said, "Stay with the client, rather than with a theory" (p. 57). If a clinician is intent on working with teenagers, there are many qualities that are prerequisite for helping today's youth. For example, a therapist's mission is to dilute the impact of trauma on a young person's life, in other words, to normalize the adolescent's world. However, the therapist *must not be neutral.* The therapist, in his or her own heart, must care and must always provide a safe, predictable, loving atmosphere for the youth.

Therapists need to care for these youths unconditionally. Therefore, if a therapist is continually struggling with countertransference issues that cannot be overcome, then he or she should not work with this population. For example, a therapist who has always been troubled by his or her own father's use of abusive language and finds that he or she is unable to deal effectively with the emotions that resurface when a youth uses that language in sessions, should consider his or her own inability to form a therapeutic alliance. The therapist may be better off requesting that another therapist work with the teenager. A therapist should be able to accept and help each youth understand all of his or her adaptive responses and accompanying disguises.

It is not easy to comprehend the memory distortions and perceptions of traumatic childhood experiences. A youth's memory of traumatic events may be fragmented into digestible parts. A therapist treating adolescents should not adjust or tamper with the memory of an adolescent. These memories are what the teenager can live with successfully. The therapist should rarely interpret, allowing instead the youth to draw his or her own conclusions. Remember, the teenager is the hero and survivor. The youth has often transcended the physical or sexual abuse and/or the psychological maltreatment. The meaning of child abuse to an adolescent must come from the adolescent's alliance with his or her self, and validate the strength already manifested through the endurance of the child abuse. The youth must do the work. However, success is dependent in part upon the degree of trust established, which in the end determines how much attention the teenager pays to therapeutic guidance. Therapists need to remember that the youth is the expert, the eyewitness to his or her own derailment. Therapists get their knowledge of the youth's life secondhand and sometimes thirdhand. The degree of the teenager's acting out may be mitigated by the success of the new relationship with the therapist.

Therapists need to be optimistic, and capable of believing in the recovery of a youth subjected to atrocities that are often so hideous that they are impossible to verbalize. They must believe the foundations for development can be established in adolescence. These teenagers can make recoveries from trauma regardless of when they start healing.

Holding true to psychoanalytic theory that suggests that these young people suffer from personality disorders will not likely help these young people. A successful therapist will invest in the theory that replaces the diagnosis of personality disorder with a framework that suggests the youth has suffered an interruption in development. These detailed interruptions can be cast along the lines of Freudian psychosexual development, Erikson's psychosocial development, Kohlberg's moral development, or Piaget's intellectual development (cited in Smart and Smart, 1967). One of the more obvious examples is the interruption of "basic trust" in the first two years of a young child's life spent with an abusive mother. Borrowing from these leaders may be helpful in identifying stages of development in young people, because, depending on when the trauma occurred, the normal processes such as sexual development, memory development, or social development have been disturbed.

Rather than trying to break the spirit of a youth who has been traumatized, therapists need to fortify it. Honoring the youth's resilience and courage and redirecting the energy behind the youth's anger to help him or her see the world as a more stable and as a safer place in which to live is part of the therapeutic process. Therapists *must not* take control away from these youths, except when they present a danger to themselves or others. Teenagers must learn to master their own ability to deal with their own histories. Their struggles with their own burdens of freedom are their ultimate social responsibilities. Therapists must be strong enough to share and absorb some of the overwhelming pain they endure. Supportive supervision, consultation, and/or psychotherapy for therapists in this field are essential. Youths integrate suffering very slowly, in tiny doses, and therefore the therapist must constantly validate their courage. These young people will eventually want to tell their stories with honor and dignity—but only when they are ready.

A therapist must never be desensitized to the pain these youths have endured. In addition, a therapist must have acquired a degree of maturity and mastery of his or her own story. If a therapist has not mastered his or her own traumatic story and works with a youth who has a similar traumatic story, the therapist may not be strong enough to help the youth. In fact, the youth may sense a need to care for the therapist. Again, if this occurs, a therapist should refer the youth to another therapist.

Last, skilled therapists treating adolescents must believe young people are central in importance in America. Youths deserve hearty environments, and adolescence is not too late to attain that kind of environment. Therapists must understand that adults often represent to youths a self-centered and desensitized generation that has recklessly squandered and even damaged both its human and non-human resources. Because this vision of adults is commonly held by some youths today, particularly traumatized ones, adult interventions with young people need to be ethical, real, and enacted with love and understanding. The following examples illustrate specific interventions with young people traumatized by child abuse. All preserve the power of youths. These interventions will suggest an authentic relationship model of therapy:

Fred's Story:

One morning, Fred came into a therapist's office, agitated, unable to discuss his anxiety. When Fred found it impossible to regulate his hyperarousal, he announced he was "taking off." The therapist let him know that he wished to go with him; out the door he darted with the therapist trailing behind. After they had walked quickly down the street for some time, the therapist asked Fred if he could take him to breakfast. Very surprised, he responded, "Sure!" Several pancakes later, Fred was relaxed enough to let the therapist know what was happening so he could assist.

Deborah's Story:

Deborah was a beautiful, eighteen-year-old young woman who had a long history of attempting suicide. Several of the attempts had been almost lethal. The therapist worked closely with her for about six months. Deborah attempted suicide again. She called the therapist about 2:00 a.m. after she had been drinking for hours and had ingested half a bottle of barbituates. As the therapist screamed at her over the phone to give her address, Deborah finally mumbled some numbers and a street, then passed out on the phone. The therapist sent an ambulance to her home and waited for what seemed like eternity, but was in fact maybe fifteen minutes. A police officer informed the therapist that the paramedics were with the young woman. She lived, and the therapist was at her bedside when she awakened. Deborah's first words to the therapist were, "I love you." The therapist's first words to her were, "Bulls—."

After working with the young woman for another year, watching her steadily improve, the therapist asked her what she believed was the most helpful part of the relationship. Deborah replied, "You know that time in the hospital after I had tried to kill myself, when you said, 'Bulls—,' that was the turning point. I realized that I didn't know how to love. . . . Well, I am no longer suicidal, I have learned to love." She has not attempted to harm herself again.

Jim's Story:

This is an example of "no words therapy." Jim, a foster son, had a fiery temper. Late one night he crashed his fist through a hallway wall. The therapist asked his foster parents not to speak with him about the incident. They were instructed to repair the wall the next day when Jim was out. The foster parents honored the suggestion, and only one other time in three years did Jim become so angry that he punched a hole in the wall. Again, they did not confront him. When a youth blasts his fist through a wall, he is clearly and loudly telling you his immediate story.

Eric's Story:

Eric was a young man in day treatment. He was a sensitive young person who intensely felt the pressures of life. He and the staff with whom he was working created the art of "paper-wad therapy." When Eric was struggling to regulate the magnitude of his feelings, he took an entire pad of letter-sized paper and carefully peeled off each sheet. After tearing off a sheet, he crumpled it and tossed it across the room. He could toss the sheet with great force or merely drop it. The resulting design in the room always gave a visual representation of his mood.

Jessica's Story:

This example of adolescent relationship therapy with a young girl entailed turning the therapist's office into a beauty parlor. The therapist took the risk to let Jessica restyle her hair in the therapist's office, with spray-on colors, mousse, and hair spray. Jessica discovered that the therapist could keep up with her, and cared to.

Kenny's Story:

This intervention involved a recommendation to Kenny's foster mother, who was having problems with him running away. The therapist suggested that the next time she suspected Kenny was unhappy enough to dart into the night, she should pack up a small duffel herself and let him know she wished to go with him. She followed through and the result was quite wonderful. Kenny had no idea what he would do with his foster mother on the run with him, and decided he had better stay home.

Analyzing the above interventions from a clinical perspective, they provide an authentic relationship complement to the fragmenting or shattering self of the adolescent, so common in young people who have been traumatized by child abuse. Although the relationship the therapist builds with a traumatized teen is very important, equally important is that of assisting caretakers. Caretakers are key in the creation and maintenance of a holding environment, to be discussed in depth in the next chapter.

There are eight very specific tasks therapists can use in helping parents sustain their courage in mastering child abuse: (1) teach parents to maintain safety at all times under all circumstances; (2) help parents to uncover the complexity of the configurations in the family that led to the abuse; (3) promote the realistic understanding of roles and expectations of each family member; (4) expect interactions between family members that preserve the civil rights of each member; (5) teach great family interactions; (6) educate parents on the traumatic impact of child abuse, the spectrum of adaptive responses, and goals of recovery; (7) refer family members to specialized treatment, such as alcohol treatment, as necessary; and (8) help interagency collaboration by adding supports for a family.

Each family's resolution of child abuse will be different because of the differing attitudes, mores, and character development of the members, and also because of the degree of hurt inflicted upon individuals and the family structure. Support the diversity of resolutions. The family structure may need to change forever. Helping the family establish new load-bearing supports for the changed structure is often needed but not encouraged due to territorial considerations of different agencies. Encourage agency professionals to form partnerships with family members.

Many theories about caring for teenagers distract adults from carrying out their primary nurturing responsibilities. Some professionals espouse tough love, others promote rigid systems of consequences, others recommend teenagers should have more freedom to make mistakes. Two primary tenets of parenting must be practiced: dedication, and the creation of a safe environment. Without these features of parenting in place, all other creative ideas will lose power. For example, if an adult wishes to help a teenager with his or her homework on a consistent basis, the adult may have to sacrifice significant personal time and interests to honor this commitment. The degree of dedication and safety displayed by adults toward youths will influence young people's mental health forever.

Chapter 8

CASTT: Child Abuse
Specific Treatment of Trauma

A HOLDING ENVIRONMENT

Children do not develop in a vacuum. They are influenced by the people with whom they are raised, the people from whom they are descended, and the myriad of social factors to which they are exposed. In some way, each person with whom a child comes in contact, either directly or indirectly, has the potential to affect the child's life.

The environment recommended for teenagers who have experienced child abuse is founded on the theory of a holding environment, defined by D. W. Winnicott (1965) in his remarkable book, *The Maturational Processes and the Facilitating Environment.* Winnicott's work is based on observations of mother-infant relationships; however, his work is the foundation piece for adolescent recovery from the trauma of child abuse. According to Winnicott, "The term 'holding' is used . . . to denote not only the actual physical holding of the infant, but also the total environmental provision prior to the concept of living with," (p. 43). Therefore, an environment of physical and psychological safety must be created before dependency, trust and attachment can be accomplished. "The holding environment therefore has as its main function the reduction to a minimum of impingements to which the infant must react with resultant annihilation of personal being" (p. 47). In a holding environment, "The infant becomes able to experience anxiety associated with disintegration" (p. 44). In the infant's memory bank is registered the needed comfort and care to develop an integrated personality structure. In this environment comes "the dawn of intelligence" (p. 45). This environment provides teaching for "being alone in the presence of someone" (p. 33). All of these accomplishments are milestones to health, but the main function of the holding environment is to provide safety. Psychological and physical safety must be restored through the therapeutic process to help an adolescent recover from child abuse.

A hearty, curative environment can be created in an outpatient office, a classroom, a hospital, a day treatment center, a birth home, or a foster home. The length of time a teenager needs to dwell in such an environment is related to the days and years, during which the young person experienced a savage environment. This curative environment is safe, predictable, clean, and energetic. It has warmth, cheerful colors, flowers, plants, interesting reading, soft music, comfortable furniture in good repair. Like an infant, a teenager experiences the spirit of the environment first, then she or he experiences people.

However, many of the environments we offer to teenagers for the purpose of rehabilitation are often equivalent to or worse than the ones they have already experienced. It is hard to imagine how an adolescent who has been traumatized by child abuse can be expected to change his or her life when the youth is placed into a coercive, punitive, controlling, demeaning environment, such as a detention center or a seclusion room in a hospital. A young person is not likely to fantasize a hearty environment while he or she is living themes from a Stephen King novel. No wonder recidivism of previously detained youths is so high. Savage environments cripple prosocial development.

Ken's Story

This true story brings much to bear on the concept of a spiritually corrective environment, or a hearty environment. The savage environment from which this fourteen-year-old needed to recover involved unpredictable beatings with a belt from a stepfather. By the time his birth mother was strong enough to leave the abuser, Ken's development had been shattered. He was joyriding, staying out all night, misusing drugs, and was unwilling to connect with his formerly trusted birth mother and father. After several months of day treatment intervention, his therapist recommended psychiatric hospitalization or a residential treatment center. Wisely, Ken's parents, rather than institutionalize him, sent him to a lovely, highly structured, private boarding school. In a two-year period, Ken grew into a stable, self-confident young man. He even became fluent in a foreign language. Unfortunately, such interventions are not economically accessible to everyone.

PEER GROUP RECOVERY AND GROWTH

Being part of a community—a family—whose members understand the individual is the most powerful tool in adolescent recovery from psychological trauma. The phenomenon of healing in large groups has probably existed since the beginning of time, but until the last several decades, these gatherings may not have been recognized as such. The gatherings at the Compassion Center after the Oklahoma City federal building bombing were dedicated to adapting and healing.

Another illustration was the 1992 gathering of forty or more survivors of the seizure of the *USS Pueblo* in 1968 by North Korea. This gathering, held in Pueblo, Colorado over the Fourth of July weekend, was the fourth since their release after almost a year of captivity. These captives shared stories of heroism that included enduring being spit upon and beaten by rifle butts. They understood each other and could attend to the ongoing healing process from such a frightening event.

In the *Los Angeles Times,* Doug Smith (1986) wrote an article titled, "Bond Unites Children of Holocaust." He reported on a group of adults who were children of Holocaust victims and described them as feeling like "phantom siblings" and that "They feel like the family that they have all done without." At the time of Smith's writing, the group included 150 members. One member, Daisy Miller, described group members' feelings that were found to be remarkably similar to those of the adolescents at the day treatment program, Hampden Academy, in the early 1990s, where the CASTT model was developed. She remarked,

> In almost every group there is that feeling of exhilaration that comes from the feeling of finally being accepted. . . . We come from very diverse walks of life. And yet we have this strange

warmth and closeness which transcends all the other stuff.
(Smith, 1986, p. 1)

Teenagers who have experienced the trauma of child abuse have
some feelings similar to those who have experienced other kinds of
hostage or terrorist situations. Even though the Holocaust exemplified
genocide, the most extreme form of oppression and violence known to
humankind, utilizing some of the same principles used with Holocaust
survivors may well be of benefit when working with traumatized
adolescents. Any comparisons used here are not meant to imply that
the experience of child abuse is the same as the experience of the
Holocaust. Each population of survivors has separate needs, even
where there is overlap. Indeed, there is often considerable variation
in the responses of two people with similar life experiences.

Both Holocaust survivors and teenage child abuse survivors are
naturally and spontaneously homogeneous beings. A facilitator
needs only to bring these people together, provide them with a
working structure, and then watch the healing. The facilitator can be
a minister, a teacher, a boy's or girl's club leader, or an athletic
coach. A holding environment can be created in many places.

Like Holocaust survivors, teenagers who have been traumatized
by child abuse believe there is a chasm between themselves and the
rest of humanity. They have been made to feel like second-class
citizens resulting from the atrocity and indignity of persecution and
rejection. Their sense of living in a world that is predictable and
safe has vanished forever. For both groups, the identities of the
members have been boosted by similar psychological legacies.
Jews were viewed as bad and dangerous by the Nazis—deserving of
being locked away or killed. Teenagers who act out the suffering of
child abuse are viewed by many adults in society as deserving of the
same fate. Both the survivors of the Holocaust and teenagers who
suffer from child abuse have experienced incidents that are cata-
strophic and beyond their ability to control. The incidents reach the
traumatic range due to their magnitude and intensity as well as their
unmasterability. Too often, members of both groups struggle with
fragments of traumatic experiences—such as in flashbacks of the
scenes—and are unable to integrate them into a healthy mind-set.
Their memories are beset with evil thoughts. They do not need to

fantasize about evil, they have experienced evil! Therefore, reconstructing events in their lives is painful, difficult, and takes great courage—the same courage it took for their initial survival.

Child abuse in the United States is a tragedy. Eric Easton's (1991) *Child Protection Report Letter* announced and underlined a figure of 2.6 million reported cases of child abuse. The American Humane Association (1995) published the following:

> In *Child Maltreatment 1993: Reports from the States to the National Center on Child Abuse and Neglect*, released in April 1995 by NCANDS, the estimated number of children reported for child abuse and/or neglect was 2.9 million, with approximately 1,018,692 of these cases substantiated (confirmed) for abuse after investigation. (Because this report contains detailed data that requires more time to analyze, 1993 is the latest year for which these types of statistics are available.) (Fact Sheet #1, p. 1)

These statistics are staggering, and underline a significant tragedy that unfortunately is continuing to take place in this country.

Helping young people to recover from destruction they have experienced involves facilitating the healing of the last and probably most harmful similarity which they share with Holocaust survivors—their silence. They are hidden heroes because they silently draw on internal strength to overcome the feelings of inferiority and shame that accompany abuse. Community meetings at the Hampden Academy day treatment program were often the first time these young students had moved out of their isolated inner worlds and broken their silence. The consistency of a group membership provided the needed structure that had been fragmented in the past. As with Holocaust survivors, these young people have often lost multiple family members. The feelings of shame are bad enough when they tell their stories, but sadly, listeners will often not believe them.

> Holocaust survivors were rarely believed by the North Americans whom they came to live amongst. Child survivors were discouraged from speaking by caretakers; this could have been important to their recovery by contributing to undoing the years of deceit which had been necessary to their survival. In

the ghetto and in hiding, children found it necessary to steal, to lie about their age, etc. They were often terrorized into silence. (Kinsler, 1990a, p. 8)

In the late 1980s and early 1990s, the teachers and therapists at Hampden Academy worked very hard to establish the atmosphere of a holding environment. The concept of educational family meant that love and caring were part of the curriculum for six hours, a kind of kinesthetic or affective education. The notion of community government was encouraged through the opportunity for daily, safe, free expression. The model created at Hampden is portable.

Each morning, all members of the Hampden family, numbering about thirty-five, met first period in the living room. All offices surrounded the living room, creating an architectural holding environment. There were no long hallways at Hampden Academy. The living room, with its couches and chairs, generated a feeling that was central to the safety and comfort of the Hampden students. During this first meeting of the day, students and staff were free to address one of three categories for discussion: comforts, concerns, and cares. An example of a comfort was a young woman consoling her mother who had been evicted from her apartment; a care was one student confronting another for cursing at the teacher in math class.

A concern mentioned often was that of the prevalence of violence in the lives of young people. During one morning meeting, one of the teachers began a discussion by recapping a *60 Minutes* report by Morley Safer (1992) on the "epidemic" violence in the lives of young people. Mr. Safer reported that guns were the single biggest killer of young black men, and that in 1990, 2,000 young blacks had been murdered. He went on to report that, in 1991: it was estimated that 90,000 young people had carried guns to school; in Boston alone, police had taken 1,155 firearms from the streets; and that a three-year-old had taken a gun to day care. One of the students suggested that gang members often carry guns for protection. The discussion gravitated to another teacher who quoted John Holt (1969): "The fundamental educational problem of our time is to find ways to help children grow into adults who have no wish to do harm" (p. 116).

At the end of the day the group met again, bound by another triadic conceptual structure. Freedom of speech was broken down into the following categories: announcements, issues, and appreciations. These group meetings provided a spirit of respect, and provided the glue that kept the holding environment for the students strong and secure.

Announcements included letting students know when assignments were due, field trips planned, and visits by guest speakers. "Issues" became a topic that provided many benefits for all of us. Typical issues could be anything from a recommendation to the staff to relax discipline, to a request to allow students to wear hats in school.

Appreciations were marvelous. They ranged from teachers telling students how wonderful their class work had been, to students telling teachers that they were not "all bad." In addition, this was the time when therapists could compliment students for the hard work they put into their recovery process (or therapy), and students were able to thank therapists for the guidance.

Every Friday, for ninety minutes, students wishing feedback on personal growth addressed the Hampden family. This was a risk-taking process. The student wishing for feedback fielded comments from often over twenty people. A wonderful example was a four-teen-year-old girl who lived with her single-parent mother who often had to work nights as a nurse at the local hospital. The young girl loved to have her friends over when her mother was gone. The girl asked for help in being more self-disciplined. The final resolution was that one of the students made herself available by phone to help give the girl strength to say "No" to other friends.

Last, during the traditional school year, the group met after lunch. This group varied each day. Some of the more creative examples of how the Hampden family used this thirty-minute period were listening to feelings-laden music and watching film segments that were trauma related. A popular song with the students was "Eye of the Hurricane" by David Wilcox (1989). The image created is that of a young girl on a motorcycle. The lyrics include the following lines:

> Tell the truth—explain to me how you got this need for speed.
> She laughed and said it just might be the next best thing to love.

After listening to the song, questions such as, "Why is speed the next best thing to love?" were asked.

Parts of a favorite film, *Ordinary People* (1980), were shown with caretaker permission. The film's plot concerns a teenager's difficulty in dealing with his brother's accidental death, for which he feels blame. After his brother's death, the teenager becomes suicidal—not believing his own life is important. His mother is unable to show him compassion or to help with his pain because she cannot recover from her son's death either. Suicide attempts and contemplation of suicide are, unfortunately, close friends of day treatment students. Also, the death of a family member is a painful challenge for these youths.

Other group models found to be helpful to teenagers struggling with traumatic stress are traditional art therapy groups, student-run advice groups, and debate groups. There seem to be unlimited possibilities for group participation. The vehicles or themes used to carry a large group, in our eyes, are secondary to the kinds of connections that are made in these groups. This is particularly true when these connections serve as a front-line defense against terror.

DEVELOPMENTAL THEORIES

In infancy, a baby gives unconditional love. When a child matures, the process of being unprotected from extreme hardship and betrayal dissolves this unconditional love into mistrust. (Bowlby, 1973; Erikson, 1950). The importance of a consistent, loving caretaker was manifested in each of the following two studies.

Ainsworth Study

Infants were observed both when separated from their mothers and when their mothers were present in the room. When their mothers were absent, the observers noticed stress in each of the infants (Bell, 1970).

Tizard and Tizard Study

Two-year-olds being cared for in residential nurseries were compared to two-year-olds living in their own homes and in intact families. The researchers studied attachment and fear symptoms in both groups. The children living in the residential group were found to show more fear of strangers and more anxiety related to attachment (Tizard and Tizard, 1971).

Implications

The implications of these studies and of Bowlby's (1973) work are significant to therapists for understanding the difficulties in forming a trusting relationship with an adolescent who has been traumatized by child abuse. When these youths are growing up, often:

> The very existence of care taking and supportive figures is unknown; . . . the whereabouts of such figures has been constantly uncertain. For many more, the likelihood that a care taking figure would respond in a supportive and protective way has been at best hazardous and at worst nil. When such people become adults it is hardly surprising that they have no confidence that a care taking figure will ever be truly available and dependable. Through their eyes the world is seen as comfortless and unpredictable; and they respond by either shrinking from it or doing battle with it. (Bowlby, 1973, p. 208)

CHILD ABUSE SPECIFIC TREATMENT OF TRAUMA

Overview

In the process of developing rapport with a traumatized youth, it is often helpful to draw a parallel between a physical injury, such as a broken limb, and the emotional injuries stemming from child abuse. The CASTT acronym was created in order to facilitate the understanding of this analogy for young people.

A cast is essentially used as a holding environment for a broken limb. It provides support and stability while the bone and surrounding tissue heal. When that degree of support and structure is no longer needed, the cast is removed. The process of rebuilding the strength of the limb then begins: at times through physical therapy, at other times by attempting to continue with previously experienced activities. When the pain is unbearable, increased support may be added. Even after healing has occurred, the particular bone involved will likely be somewhat vulnerable to future injury. Attention should be paid to reducing the risk of this happening, as well as watching for warning signs of renewed damage. In other words, it may require some degree of lifetime attention in order to assure the fullest possible functioning.

Oftentimes, when a young person is abused, no one else sees the damage. When young people are emotionally insulted and beaten down, they often feel so bad about themselves that they do not speak. After they have been physically or sexually abused and have recovered from physical wounds, the psychological wounds remain. They often believe they are "bad kids." The impact of abuse may fester if ignored. A sort of emotional cast may be needed in order for the youth to begin to heal. This may involve physically removing the child from a locale of abuse, or providing an adequate emotional holding environment within which the youth can begin to recover. The many groups of adult survivors of horrible kinds of abuse validate that the pain can linger for years.

In adolescence, mistrust acts as a catalyst that attacks meaningful relationships with adults. Therapists working with traumatized adolescents need to develop a sharp understanding of how teenagers adapt to past trauma as well as to ongoing trauma. Therapists must also not delude themselves that a therapeutic relationship will develop immediately—a trusting relationship with a traumatized adolescent will take time.

The American Psychiatric Association (1994) stated the following:

> The essential feature of Posttraumatic Stress Disorder is the development of characteristic symptoms following exposure to an extreme traumatic stressor involving direct personal experience of an event that involves actual or threatened death or serious injury, or other threat to one's physical integrity; or witnessing an event that involves death, injury, or a threat to the physical integrity of another person; or learning about unexpected or violent death, serious harm, or threat of death or injury experienced by a family member or other close associate. (p. 424)

Because an experience or series of experiences is markedly distressing implies that an individual will struggle with integrating the input. When the input from one's environment is too great to integrate into one's personality development at any age, one must adapt somehow.

We believe that in adolescence there are six very specific adaptive responses to the trauma of child abuse that are manageable for youths, and twelve adaptations that are symptomatic of struggles for which they need help (discussion in detail will follow). All of these adaptations are explainable and often necessary for young people to survive child abuse. The challenge to the professional is not to stigmatize the struggles of young people, but to provide young people with help. Currently in Colorado, for adolescents to qualify for services in the schools and in community mental health centers, diagnostic profiles must be provided. The more detailed and professionally written the clinical reports are, the more a youth gains interagency recognition. Legitimizing more innocuous, humane descriptions of young people is difficult. For example, diagnosing young people who have experienced child abuse with ACA (Adapting to Child Abuse) would be professionally unacceptable. Because there is no such diagnosis, the authors have relied on the diagnosis of PTSD. PTSD does imply a mental disorder and recommended treatment. Under Colorado Law 27-10, a person suffering from mental illness has "A substantial disorder of the cognitive, volitional or emotional processes that grossly impairs judgment or capacity to recognize reality or to control behavior." Therefore, the following CASTT model can be implied as viable treatment.

The CASTT Model in Action

When using the Child Abuse Specific Treatment of Trauma model, it is important to give careful thought in making a differential diagnosis. For example, traumatized youths, when experiencing anxiety, may shut down. Parents, teachers, and therapists may perceive this shut-down as noncompliant or uncooperative and defiant behavior—earning the diagnosis of oppositional defiant disorder (Perry, 1993b). For example, in 1994, we worked with a number of young teenage girls who had been raped. These girls had been commonly diagnosed with bipolar disorder in previous therapies and had been ineffectively placed on lithium. Their mood struggles had not been affected by the medication. Prior treatment had failed to focus on the traumatic experience of rape.

CASTT is a model for assessment and treatment of traumatic stress responses during adolescence based on knowledge of prior child abuse in a teenager's life. Before working with the CASTT model, we recommend that therapists complete the following protocols in order. These are stages of mental health assessment.

1. Emergency needs of the youth or safety implications
2. Organic brain damage, physical head trauma, and other, possibly immediate, medical needs
3. Presence of a major mental illness (other than PTSD)
4. Culturally-specific adaptations
5. Ecological factors

It is only at this *fifth* stage of assessment that the impact of child abuse is considered. We cannot emphasize strongly enough the phenomenon of increasing numbers of adolescents appearing in the multiagency net with comorbid features. A teenager is often brought to the attention of mental health workers, caseworkers, and attorneys with features of depression, run-away behavior, and substance abuse. Therefore, making an accurate assessment of the difficulties of teenagers is often complicated. These assessments often need to be made by interdisciplinary teams, or at least by a professional who has cross-training.

The process of treatment with a young teenage client who has been traumatized by child abuse is threefold. The first duty is to educate the youth in the dynamics of traumatic stress and the possible development of a spectrum of post-traumatic stress symptoms or adaptive responses. The second step is to help the youth recover from the ravages of child abuse. The therapist makes a clear statement to the youth that the therapist understands the civil rights of the youth have been violated, and that traumatic stress from child abuse is inextricably linked to human rights violations. After the youth has been given a written copy of the Clinical Matrix and a copy of the CASTT goals, the therapeutic work together shifts. The youth is then assisted in putting in place an internal structure of principles by which he or she is willing to make decisions and live. If a young person leaves therapy without a code of ethics and lives an unprincipled life—a life very similar to his or her early childhood—the therapy has likely not been helpful.

Teenagers, as well as younger children, can understand their need to shift from the corrupt world of child abuse to the healthy world of preserving human dignity. The dimension of therapy that plays a vital role in addressing the needed moral shift in development is the presence of a holding environment. Wraparound service models have noted success accomplishing this task with teenagers. An example would be a sixteen-year-old held safely by a loving caretaker, by therapists and teachers at an excellent day treatment program, by a caseworker who gives the caretaker lots of support, and by a tracker from a probation department. These young people must take from therapeutic interventions the best of human values and develop the convictions to live by them.

The third step is to open the door to doing trauma work. Specific trauma work with teenagers is arduous. This is the process whereby the therapist carefully helps the youth shed some of his or her adaptive responses. As much as possible, the therapist should consistently try to reflect back upon the former heroism of the young person. Again, the reexperiencing of pain from severe child abuse is almost always overwhelming. Many young people, even with help, do not have the internal strength to do this work. Unless a youth is high-risk in terms of surviving his or her adolescence, taking this work slowly or even delaying it may be the most therapeutic choice. Therefore, the third process may be only to introduce the dynamics of trauma work educationally, and then let it go. The teenager must be in charge of this process and the therapist a guide.

We have developed CASTT Intake Information forms (Appendix A) to record historical data to clarify traumatic experiences. However, there are other options for gathering information that specifically promote relationship building, such as: narratives written by the teenager, or by the therapist with the youth as the editor; stories told into a tape recorder; stories enacted through plays or in front of a video camera; or by creating sequential drawings to form a visual narrative. These stories are too big for these young people to divulge at once; therefore, narrative work must be undertaken cautiously and in stages.

When a youth is diagnosed with PTSD, the youth's degree of functioning is described using the six continua depicted in Figure 8.1. The PTSD diagnosis provides the most realistic and honor-preserving framework from which to begin CASTT.

The six continua outlined in Figure 8.1 are descriptive and based on the observation of approximately 300 teenagers in the day treat-

FIGURE 8.1. A Clinical Matrix for CASTT: Six Continua Describing Adolescent Adaptation to Traumatic Stress*

Natural Responses to Traumatic Stress that can keep teenagers safe	Responses to Traumatic Stress that can place teenagers at risk	(ARES) Adolescent Responses to Extreme Stress that place a teenager and/or the community at risk
1. NUMBED RESPONSE	ALEXITHYMIA	HIGH SUICIDE RISK
• Afraid to feel intensity of feelings associated with traumatic events. • Tunes out content related to traumatic experiences.	• Inability to give verbal symbols for feelings. • Inability to transform and regulate emotions mentally. • Change in body chemistry.**	• Because unable to transform emotions into positive action, quits—sees life as hopeless; foreshortened sense of future. • Diminished interests and initiative. • Self-mutilation. • Change in body chemistry.**
2. HYPERVIGILANCE	24-HOUR MAD WATCH	PARANOIA
• Feeling unprotected. • On guard under certain circumstances.	• Feeling personally vulnerable. • On guard most of the time.	Feeling others motivated to cause harm.
3. HYPERAROUSAL	HYPERACTIVITY	OUT-OF-CONTROL BEHAVIOR
• Easily agitated. • Struggles to concentrate in school. • Change in body chemistry.**	• Anxious, restless. • Poor ability to concentrate. • Change in body chemistry.**	• Aggressive. • Apt to commit a crime. • Explosive behavior. • Change in body chemistry.**

152

	MODIFIED REPLAY	ACTUAL REPLAY	OBSESSIVE REENACTMENT
4.	• Simple practice and mastery as in play therapy. • Daydreams. • Symbolic behaviors.	• Learned behavior. • Identity reinforcement. • Sudden acting out of trauma or re-experiencing. • Flashbacks.	• Wanting to feel control over own life for self-efficacy. • Flashbacks.
	HEIGHTENED CREATIVITY	CREATIVE INDEPENDENCE	DISSOCIATION
5.	Original dress, language, music, dance.	• Traditional boundaries weakened. • Intergenerational misunderstanding.	• Emotional and cognitive separation from self. • Amnesia—believing it did not happen. • Identity confusion.
	EARLY EMOTIONAL SEPARATION FROM ADULTS	PHYSICAL SEPARATION FROM ADULTS	DRUG DEPENDENCE; UNSAFE SEXUAL BEHAVIOR
6.	• Relationships with significant adults disrupted and interrupted. • Adaptation to adult betrayal.	• Running away. • Joining gangs. • Hospitalization. • Foster care. • Jail. • Drug abuse to regulate emotions.	• Chemical dependency. Looking for emotional comfort that can be controlled. • Teen pregnancy.

*This description does not match DSM-IV.
**Recent research showing evidence of biochemical changes in people with PTSD.

ment facility of Hampden Academy over a nine-year period. Moving across Continuum 1, a youth showing the normal numbed response to, for example, continual beatings from a parent, becomes unable to tolerate and transform emotions into positive action or thought and thus gives up the struggle. The adolescent sees his or her life as hopeless and feels helpless in handling the pressures of school or a job. With this abbreviated sense of future, the youth becomes a high risk for suicide.

We have applied the term *alexithymia* to the numbing response in teenagers (Taylor, 1989). The application of this term represents a far-reaching hypothesis of ours. However, we have observed many young people with child abuse histories not being able to talk about their feelings at the time of abuse, and not being able to describe their feelings about current situations. It is hoped that future research will support this usage. This concept suggests an inability to verbalize feelings. To demonstrate are observations of teenagers, who, while the tears are streaming down their faces, insist that they are not sad. They will purge emotions, however, as part and parcel of one or more of the other responses in Continuum 1. These youths are normally unable to validate their pain in any verbal form. They just know they hurt. Often suicidal gestures, such as self-inflicted cuts and other self-mutilations, are external ways of giving recognition to the suffering that they are afraid to feel emotionally. Youths assessed on Continuum 1 are often misinterpreted by professionals as being unable to attach to an adult. These youths often demonstrate alexithymic symptoms through poor eye contact, flat or inappropriate affect, and inability to understand their own feelings or the feelings of others. Yet, many youths seen as alexithymic can and do attach to consistent, loving caretakers.

Continuum 2 describes degrees of hypervigilance. On the statue in front of the National Archives Building in Washington DC, is a quote from Thomas Jefferson, "Eternal Vigilance Is the Price Of Liberty." Those teenagers who have had the fortitude to endure and recover from traumatic stress are more likely to feel safe and free, but the price, as Jefferson said, is eternal vigilance. Those who have not recovered remain unsure of the real motives and behaviors of others and at times their judgments becomes impaired, and they exhibit fears that border on the level of paranoia. One student at

Hampden Academy very insightfully termed the hypervigilance of another student as his classmate's "twenty-four-hour mad watch."

Continuum 3, hyperarousal, is closely linked to the numbed response. As teenagers struggle to regulate and identify intense emotions, they commonly act on them, manifesting agitation and aggressive behavior. Traumatized adolescents easily shift into a behavioral mode that can be characterized as "out of control." There are a number of reasons for this shifting of gears. First, their body chemistry changes. There is increasing evidence that a change takes place in the behavior of neurotransmitters in the nervous system of traumatized individuals—norepinephrine, dopamine, and serotonin, to name three. These changes may be programmed during the years of abuse. Dr. Bruce Perry of Baylor College of Medicine stated the following:

> Understanding the traumatized child requires recognition of a key principle of developmental neurobiology: the brain develops and organizes as a reflection of developmental experience, organizing in response to the pattern, intensity and nature of sensory and perceptual experience . . . The traumatized child's template for brain organization is the stress response. (Perry, 1993a, p. 196)

Dr. Perry went on to say, "The stressful experience, via a cascade of neurochemical events, alters the microenvironmental milieu of the central nervous system (CNS), resulting in altered gene expression" (Perry, 1993a, p. 196).

More easily identified symptomatology includes an elevated heart rate. According to Dr. Perry, in the early 1990s, "Our work . . . has demonstrated that traumatized children, even when they are 'behaving' and acting like 'good kids,' will have profound physiological hyperactivity, such as heart rates above 120 even while asleep" (Perry, 1993b, p. 203). Pharmacotherapy can play an important role in helping with biochemical change. "Medications help buffer the dysregulation and sensitization seen in the brain stem and midbrain neurotransmitter systems involved in mediating PTSD systems" (Perry, 1993b, p. 205).

A second reason for the uncontrollable behavior of some teenagers is that many of them who grew up in abusive, chaotic environments have become accustomed to a lifestyle with no structure, limits, or boundaries. A last reason is that many teenagers—traumatized by adult betrayal, as they perceive it—do not limit how outrageous or disrespectful their behavior becomes. In fact, they pervasively treat the values (and belongings) of these adults with great disrespect and irreverence.

In Continuum 4, reexperiencing past traumatic events in adolescence appears differently from the way it appears in adults. Teenagers who have been traumatized by child abuse often replay the trauma. They do this in an effort to master the trauma, to finally feel in control. It seems to be learned behavior, signifying a part of their identity. To illustrate this complicated dynamic is a description of the evaluation of a fifteen-year-old boy, who had stolen a gun while on vacation at his grandparents' home in another state. This boy was arrested for firing the gun in his garage three times. One of the rounds exploded through the side of the garage and became embedded in the wall of a neighbor's house. No one was hurt. The boy was charged with reckless endangerment with a deadly weapon.

One of the recommended early questions when interviewing this young man was to ask whether or not he had had another incident with a gun in his life. Very painfully, he described a childhood experience. His mother, who had endured a long history of batterings by the boy's father, during one frightful episode, yelled to her son to find help in the neighborhood. As the boy recalled, he had darted for the door as his father grabbed him and pointed a gun at his head. He recalled his father's words, "If you leave this house and tell anyone what is going on here, I'll shoot you!" The boy told us that he had stolen the gun from his grandfather to learn how to use it. The boy had no idea a bullet would go through the garage wall.

In addition, traumatized youths have distressing dreams, flashbacks, and intense discomfort at exposure to circumstances similar to traumatic events in their lives. However, as much as possible, youths will consciously block these memories of trauma. Cognitively, teenagers do not wish to reexperience trauma and will go to great lengths to consciously avoid it. From observation, the numbing response seems to be a sine qua non for boys who have been traumatized by severe, chronic child abuse. It is when these young men are unable to numb out that other adaptive patterns are employed. These youths are able to reexperience the trauma and dissociate a current replay from the past trauma.

At the extreme of Continuum 4 is obsessive reenactment. This has been observed with young girls who have, on innumerable occasions, been victims of sexual assault. These young girls often exhibit hypersexuality. Again, replaying experiences through actions is easier for a teenager than talking through incidents. These youths often have more trust in their own at-risk coping behavior than they do in a therapist's intervention.

Continuum 5 describes levels of heightened creativity. This is often characterized by bizarre dress, language, music preference, and dance interpretations. This creativity is prevalent in our public schools, which many parents view as institutions that fail to shelter and protect our youths. The hallways are flooded with teenagers, many of whom are felt to be outside of conformity.

Consider the lyrics of the song, "Mickey Mouse is Dead," by the Subhumans (1983), which describe the demise of a traditional Walt Disney cartoon hero who no longer commands the respect of many young people, "because Mommy's got no money, and Daddy is in jail."

At the extreme end of Continuum 5 is adolescent dissociation, i.e., when a youth has emotionally and cognitively separated from internal parts of himself or herself. This dynamic in adolescence is very difficult to conceptualize. In normal adolescent development, identity confusion is prevalent. Helping teenagers find themselves is normal. Teenagers are acutely conscious of the here and now. In fact, as we have described before, traumatized youths are often hypervigilant. Identifying inconsistent behavior with adolescents is much more difficult because the boundaries can be unlimited. And, it seems amnesia preserves self-esteem in adolescence. Even nontraumatized teenagers struggle to admit that anything has been bad in their lives.

Last, in Continuum 6, we have identified early separation from adults as a normal response to child abuse and other forms of betrayal by significant individuals in children's lives. Teenagers who have experienced child abuse perceive themselves as safe when on their own and/or with their peers. This is often the result of relationships that have been disrupted in some way with adults who had previously been considered as positive influences in their lives. Unlike some other professionals, we do not view these youths as incapable of attachment. There are many examples of surrogate adults who have provided safe, loving, holding environments for teenagers, in which there is an open connection. Unfortunately, if this does not occur in the community, teenagers are apt to be held in less nurturing environments, including detention centers, residential settings, and sometimes hospitals.

For many abused teens, the self-soothing mechanisms that develop within the context of loving, nurturing relationships are absent. The need to look outside of oneself may then develop. Two of the more common attempts at external self-soothing involve drug and alcohol abuse and sexual activity. The danger of becoming psychologically or physically dependent on drugs or alcohol is a reality for many youths. Choosing to use chemicals to soothe one-self initially involves volition. It is a feeling of comfort, or discomfort, which the youth is able to control. With the kind of access young people have to drugs, they can take charge of how good they feel artificially. Ironically, the drugs or alcohol may gain control through the process of chemical dependency. Substance abuse presents a horrific lure for neglected young people.

Teenage sexuality is a growing area of concern as well. The following dangers inherent in sexuality among teens applies to young people of all socioeconomic and ethnic backgrounds and sexual orientations. Sexual contact may provide a young person with a sense of connection with and caring from another person. When such a connection is present, it is not often a lasting one. Teenagers in general are not developmentally ready for a committed, reciprocal relationship with another person. In addition, the hope for such a relationship with another may indeed be just an illusion in reality. As with substance abuse, a situation in which a young person initially felt in control may drastically change. Teenagers who have previously been sexually exploited may find themselves in situations in which they are retraumatized. The internal mechanisms that alert many people to potentially dangerous situations are often not effective in traumatized people. As previously stated, hypervigilance is one potential compensation for this. The opposite difficulty, which might be termed hypovigilance, may occur as well. The ability to recognize a situation leading to harm is lacking. Indeed, many blatantly abusive situations are not labeled as such by the person who was victimized. It is not uncommon to hear young people describe situations in which they believe they have not been raped, but were forced to have sex.

Pregnancy is another prevalent result of sexual contact between teens. When young people then choose to become parents, they are suddenly thrust into a situation where they need to act as responsible adults for the sake of an infant. Many young people believe that the infant will provide them with the unconditional love and acceptance for which they have longed. To be truly needed by a helpless baby may allow the parent to no longer feel helpless herself or himself. A young parent may long for the comfort of holding a soft, endearing, beautiful infant of his or her own. Once again, the illusion of control is quickly shattered once the reality of the immense and changing needs of the child become apparent. The risk of abuse or neglect on the part of the parent is present as well, particularly if the teen does not have adequate support and resources available in his or her personal life or the community. Teen pregnancy programs can greatly mitigate some of the difficulties faced by young parents by providing nurturing adult relationships for the teens, as well as concrete instruction and support regarding child development, infant care, and educational or vocational resources.

In the not so distant past, teenage pregnancy was the most feared result of unprotected sexual intercourse among youths. In today's world, sexuality is now closely linked with disease and death. Sexually transmitted diseases, such as chlamydia, herpes, and gonorrhea can cause numerous complications, particularly when undetected. Of course, the most feared illness is AIDS, the prevalence of which is growing in both the adolescent and the heterosexual populations. Developmentally, adolescents tend to have a sense of omnipotence. AIDS is not something that many of them can relate to as a potential reality for them. The degree of misinformation regarding the ways in which sexually transmitted diseases are spread is incredible. Some teens believe that they are protected from disease if they are using birth control pills, Norplant, or similar contraceptives. Others do not realize that disease can be spread through unprotected oral sex. Such thinking may be a life-or-death mistake in today's world.

The CASTT framework validates the philosophical argument that many youths (with whom professionals have worked) who have presented a degree of derailment from social norms (legal and/or school) have experienced some trauma or series of traumata. These youths have survived in the best way possible with the resources available to them.

Youths traumatized by child abuse are special people. They have wisdom and sensitivity beyond their years. It is particularly important that they be made to feel safe through the creation of a hearty environment. It is necessary to legitimize the adaptive responses they have employed and to honor their survival work.

Unfortunately, referring to them as misguided heroes is a controversial stance from the perspective of psychoanalytic theory. The risks are (1) prematurely validating their ego strength and (2) failing to empathize with the negative emotions associated with trauma, e.g., the guilt from sexual assault (McCann and Pearlman, 1990). Our approach is initially to empathize, but also to point out the courage and incredible strength a young person has manifested to endure such hardship. By referring to these young people as heroes, the hope is to neutralize the past devastation to their self-esteem.

Figure 8.2 outlines the goals needed for adolescent recovery from traumatic stress. Teenagers begin to trust adults again only after they begin to feel a sense of mastery in their own lives (Goal 5). Once a foundation of self-confidence is established, a traumatized youth begins to connect and work with adults.

Teenagers resist doing grief work, trauma work, or the gut-wrenching aspect of working through their pain. To put it in their language, "It's not cool!" The reframing help validates the strength the youth has already displayed by surviving and transcending hardship. Youths are encouraged to continue to strengthen their alliance with themselves. In this way they are able to experience themselves "organizing around joyful, rewarding relationships and activities" (Goal 10). The framework developed may be adapted to various holding environments. For instance, a youth who has been severely abused in the first four years of life may be stabilized in an excellent foster home at the time of entering therapy. From a devel-

FIGURE 8.2. Goals for Adolescent Recovery from Traumatic Stress

1. Develop a sense of safety.
2. Identify adaptive patterns as normal; accept suffering as a part of living.
3. Identify helpfulness of adaptive patterns.
4. Identify how adaptive patterns interfere with personal control, self-discipline, and relationships.
5. Overcome helplessness: do for oneself; engage in school work; master physical challenges; and other activities.
6. Trust again—build close, meaningful relationships.
7. Work in collaboration with parents and other adults to emotionally reconnect.
8. Grieve losses and disappointments: change intense emotions, such as guilt, into sad memories.
9. Reframe and create meaning from childhood traumatic events.
10. Experience one's self as capable of organizing around joyful, rewarding relationships and activities. Create hopeful dreams and fantasies.

opmental perspective, this teenager may have begun to connect with his or her new family. With basic trust established, the youth may be struggling with autonomy and initiative issues. Because these struggles present quite a regressed picture, using a traumatic stress theory base, the youth would be struggling with Goal 5. Traumatized teenagers often manifest with school difficulties. Intelligence may be inaccurately evaluated by mastery of academic skills and knowledge. Often these young people are several grade levels behind in school. The social delays of these youths present dramatically and logically. If the disruption in development has been created by the trauma of child abuse, adult guidance from the time of the abuse forward will have a distorted integration. Therefore, learning a new, different knowledge base is often imperative. It takes time and patience from teachers and caretakers to help young people integrate new frames of reference in which knowledge will be incorporated in logical, undistorted sequences.

If young people are ready to undertake even a piece of trauma work, the work needs to begin. The more of their stories that they are able to tell (in some way), the fewer shameful burdens there will be in their lives. In particular, a self narrative provides the opportunity for a young person to gain a vision for a corrected, new frame of reference. The following story illustrates a courageous piece of trauma work, written by a fifteen-year-old girl who was sexually abused by her grandfather for over a decade. The power behind the aggression felt by traumatized youths needs to be positively redirected. This is one of the greatest challenges for adults committed to helping troubled teenagers.

Sarah's Letter *(written at age fifteen, and not mailed):*

You f—— b——, I hate you. I don't want you to call me. What you did to me for twelve years and a Saturday, really p—— me off. I hope you know I told and there's an investigation going on. I can't ever see Grandma again because of you. I am going to call my cousin, and I'm going to ask her to see if you did anything to her. If she says yes, I'm going to kill you, and I will laugh. I hope you have another heart attack and die. You don't deserve to live. You hurt me, not physically, but emotionally. I still have dreams about it. Like last night, Grandma was driving somewhere and she left me with you. We were on the deck and you took my clothes off and did it. Like a month later, I was pregnant by you.

If they do sentence you, I hope you have four decades of prison. If I had my way first, I'd nail you to the wall, then I'd hang you, then I would put you in the gas chamber, then I would give you the electric chair, and then I'd blow your brains out.

Why couldn't you just be a regular grandfather? Why did you have intercourse with me? How could you be so perverted? Why did you make me have oral sex with you? Oh, by the way, I am not going to be your wife. You know, I was afraid of you, but not anymore.

You know, I never wanted to be a girl. I always wanted to be a boy because of you. The last time I was up there, you asked me to see if I was still on my period. I felt embarrassed because I don't like talking about those things. I just want you to know that Grandma already knew. I told her two weeks ago. I know you don't care because you always ask me anyways, but I am not going to tell you anyway.

I do have a friend, and yes he is a boy, and I have told him about us. You know what he told me to do the next time you call? He told me to hang up on you. Every time, I laugh about it because I'm so hurt that I can't really express my feelings. Oh, remember that one time you said that I really wanted it. You were wrong. I never did want it. If you ever say that to me, I will just hang up the phone. I like you, but I don't like what you did to me. I mean that you hurt me really bad. I just can't believe that you did that to me. Why did you do it? Did your grandmother or grandfather do it to you, and you really didn't deal with it?

I just don't understand. I don't understand what has happened here. I started smoking because of the stress you gave me. I wish I never met you, and I wish you were never my grandfather.

Last night I had another dream about you. A dream that we were getting married. See, because of you, I don't make very good boundaries. One time another student asked me to walk out of school with her. I said, "Yes," instead of saying "No!" I got in big trouble. I had a huge lecture, and I got grounded for two months.

Thanks to you, I thought about committing suicide. My self-esteem is very low. I think everybody else is more important than myself. Everybody despises you for what you did to me. When I was in public school, I asked to ditch gym, because I didn't want to dress out for gym. Okay, you know how this has affected me.

All my life I wanted to be a kid and not a grown up. My new school has changed my life. I didn't know until now that you were a bad influence on me. It's really sad because I trusted you. I never thought that you would head me in the wrong way. I thought you were leading me in the right way of life. See, I can't trust anyone anymore because I don't know if they are going to hurt me or not. I just want you to know.

At Hampden Academy, an assignment for all students was to read *Hamlet* out loud. The quotation, "To be, or not to be, that is the question:/Whether 'tis nobler in the mind to suffer/The slings and arrows of outrageous fortune,/Or to take arms against a sea of troubles/And by opposing end them," (Shakespeare, [c. 1601] 1988, p. 64) can be applied to describe the conflicts of young people who have experienced child abuse. Questions for discussion included: What are Hamlet's clear responsibilities? As the ghost of his father has commanded, must he avenge his father's death? How frail is his mother—a woman who marries the murderer of her husband? Most of the characters in Hamlet are killed in the end of this tragedy. For the final exam after studying this play, students were asked to end the play three ways other than the way Shakespeare had. Three examples of alternative endings included the following:

1. Ophelia lives, befriends Gertrude, and together they provide guidance for Hamlet to forgive the corruption in the state. As Claudius grows older, he becomes less villainous and turns over the throne to Hamlet and his bride, Ophelia.
2. Fortinbras, King of Norway, kills Claudius, King of Denmark, in battle. Hamlet becomes the new King of Denmark.
3. Hamlet resolves in his own mind, with Horatio's guidance, not to avenge his father's death. Instead, he chooses to follow philosophical pursuits and pose no political threat to King Claudius.

Shakespeare's characters struggled to recover from trauma. Their struggles are symbolic of those of many American youths today.

Chapter 9

Constructing CASTT Teams in the Community

Implementing a CASTT model of treatment is a new way to support the mental health of traumatized teenagers. The purpose of a CASTT or a holding environment, metaphorically speaking, is to provide custom services for child and adolescent recovery from traumatic stress.

DESCRIPTION OF SERVICES

Phase One

Each community mental health center will have a therapist, most likely serving on a child-and-family team, trained in traumatic stress treatment. The therapist will also be cross-trained in systems theory and community organization. Part of the job description for the therapist will be to create a standing community team that can be mobilized within five working days. This team is not to be confused with an emergency team or a debriefing team. The standing team will consist of the mental health worker, a parent advocate, a social service caseworker, a public school liaison, a juvenile justice representative, and a psychiatrist. This team will be available to go into the home, schools, detention centers and will provide a comprehensive biological, psychological, sociological, and ecological assessment within five working days of the referral. This phase of intervention is responsible for assessment and stabilization. The CASTT matrix can be used as a clinical aid during this phase.

Phase Two

This stage will be dedicated to providing excellent, customized services to young people traumatized by child abuse. Primary caretakers and the traumatized youth will join in partnership with the standing CASTT team. The team will construct a healthy, nurturing holding environment to help a young person recover. Services that may be included as part of the design are: academic tutoring, classroom aides, after-school programs, drug/alcohol counseling, respite care, community service, probation, and mentoring, as well as specialized trauma therapy. Other supports, such as meeting with a spiritual leader, can be made available to those who choose. Nurturing holding environments provide relationships with both professionals and nonprofessionals who are rich in life experiences and wisdom. These services will need to be in place for as long as needed. No arbitrary time periods can be set. All ten goals for recovery (as presented in Chapter 8, Figure 8.2) must be addressed in Phase Two. However, these goals may not be achieved, because young people heal differently, and they also develop and grow at dissimilar rates. These services will also need to be culturally sensitive. If part of a youth's struggle is related to, for example, being gay, or a Native American, the team will need to represent specific diversities.

Phase Three

This phase will be marked by a youth feeling and acting empowered, understood, successful, and assisted. This phase will be highlighted by a youth and his or her family initiating a change in the nature of services. Relatives, friends, and/or neighbors would ease agency members out of a job by providing a strong holding environment. Professionals would play less of a direct role and more of an advocacy, resource role over time.

REFERRALS

Referrals can originate from youths and families themselves, emergency-team members in community mental health or in hospitals, doctors, social service caseworkers, school teachers, or probation officers. This list is not inclusive. The power of integrated supportive services has been demonstrated by wraparound initiatives throughout the United States. The creation of partnerships between all invested community members—including birth parents, other caretakers, school teachers, neighbors, caseworkers, and probation officers—and the creation of careful, comprehensive assessments of needs provide wonderful broad support for young people derailed by the trauma of child abuse.

CASTT TEAMS IN ACTION

Harry's Story

Harry, age sixteen, had been found by his older brother in the back yard trying to hang himself. He was hospitalized by an emergency service therapist, who then referred him to a CASTT team worker. The worker learned that both Harry and his older brother were living in an adoptive home. Harry's birth parents had been arrested five years earlier for manufacturing and selling crack cocaine. Parental rights had been terminated during their incarceration. As an infant, Harry had been badly burned on his side by scalding water that had been thrown at him. Harry had a history of several foster and group home placements before his adoption. He had been separated from his birth brother for two years, and he had a history of poor performance in high school. He also was on probation for auto theft. Even though Harry was having a difficult struggle, he was a bright, handsome boy who loved to swim. He could easily have made his high school team, but was ineligible because of his grades.

The worker contacted the adoptive parents and secured releases to speak with standing members of the team. The worker acted like a conductor of a symphony as she encouraged her team members to contact the specific important people in Harry's life. Within five working days, the CASTT team leader had visited Harry at the hospital and met with needed team members, together with Harry's adoptive parents, to complete an extensive preliminary assessment.

A hospital represents the tightest therapeutic holding environment for young people because not only is the mandate of the hospital to protect a youth, it is also to provide intensive therapeutic services. In this particular situation, the CASTT team (that included Harry, his adoptive parents, and hospital doctors) agreed that Harry needed to stay in the hospital a second week while a community CASTT was organized. During his hospitalization, Harry began to work on recovery Goals 1 through 4 (see Chapter 8, Figure 8.2). When Harry returned home, the following services were in place: one-to-one counseling daily at school, two mental health worker visits in the home per week, an after-school swimming program two days a week, and a peer academic tutor in the home one day a week to help Harry raise his grades. Because he had been placed on an antidepressant while hospitalized, he was scheduled for an appointment with a psychiatrist within seven days. Last, a therapeutic weekend foster home was made available for the first several weekends. While Harry was in this therapeutic home on the weekends, his adoptive parents received training in the CASTT model in their home.

Phase Three of treatment began after one-and-a-half years had elapsed. Harry had stopped taking medication, had discontinued using respite weekends, was swimming on his school team, and was maintaining a B average. Harry's therapist visited once a month and served mostly as a resource person. Harry's respite mother had become his mentor, speaking to him on the phone several nights a week. Harry's tutor was no longer needed.

Amy's Story

Amy was thirteen years old when she was referred to a community mental health center by her dad. Amy had been refusing to go to school and was spending each day in front of the TV set. She lived with her single parent dad who left for work early each day expecting Amy to catch the school bus. It was the day after her report card came in the mail that dad called for help. Amy had received three Fs and two Ds.

The intake worker learned from her dad that two months before the school year had started, Amy had been raped by her mother's second husband. The trial was scheduled to begin in a week. Amy was described as an outgoing, popular girl who was on the honor roll before she was raped. The intake worker contacted the CASTT worker, who immediately called her father to set up a time to meet

Amy. Then the CASTT worker mobilized the team for a meeting. The team consisted of her dad, her dad's parents and sister, and Amy's favorite teachers. The team determined that Amy would have a modified academic schedule through the trial. One of her teachers offered to pick her up in the morning for school until the trial was over. Another teacher offered to come to her house after school to tutor her on days she could not attend. The CASTT worker scheduled her for an evaluation with a child psychiatrist to assess her for depression. The CASTT worker scheduled weekly therapy for Amy and weekly consultation time with her dad. Last, meetings for specific training in the CASTT model were provided to her dad.

Phase Two lasted six months. Amy endured the trial, worked beautifully through the ten goals of recovery (Chapter 8, Figure 8.2), and began attending school again each day. By the end of the school year, Amy was back on the honor roll. In addition, the teacher who had picked her up for school for the month of the trial helped Amy courageously tell her story to her classmates.

OUTCOMES

The following outcomes have been identified in assessing the benefits of CASTT community teams:

1. Establishment of safety—no injuries to the teenager, and the teenager inflicts no injuries upon others
2. Reduction of caretaker losses—family preservation (stabilized residence and school), including long-term foster care
3. Improved school achievement—better grades
4. Improved commitment to moral behavior—reduced arrest record
5. Relief from suffering—youth and other family members report more joy in their lives

For the fifth outcome to be a reality, the team designing the CASTT must provide a spirit of love and caring. The environment must foster the dignity and courage of the young people recovering. The positive spirit of the members of the CASTT team provides hope.

Chapter 10

The Making of a Hero

Adult leaders, regardless of social roles—whether therapists, teachers, probation officers, caseworkers, or parents—are struggling to form authentic relationships with troubled youths. Policy makers are failing to establish hearty, curative environments which are known to enlighten the journeys of traumatized youths. However, in the following classic story, a bishop succeeds at both.

In drawing this book to a close, Victor Hugo's ([1862] 1982) novel, *Les Misérables,* stands out. The protagonist, Jean Valjean, experienced an epiphany based on the relationship he had with the Bishop of Digne. After enduring abject poverty and being orphaned in his formative years, Valjean, as a young adult, was brought to trial for breaking into a home and stealing a loaf of bread—to be used to feed his seven destitute nieces and nephews. He was armed with a shotgun. The disposition of his trial was for him to work five years in labor camps. The year after he was sentenced, he became part of a chain-gang. On four different occasions he tried to escape, adding years of incarceration when he was caught. The total sentence he served amounted to a staggering nineteen years.

> Moreover society as a whole had done him nothing but injury. He had seen nothing of it but the sour face which it calls justice and shows only to those it castigates. Men had touched him only to hurt him; his only contact with them had been through blows. From the time of his childhood, and except for his mother and sister, he had never encountered a friendly word or a kindly look. During the years of suffering he reached the conclusion that life was a war in which he was one of the defeated. Hatred was his only weapon, and he resolved

to sharpen it in prison and carry it with him when he left. (Hugo, [1862] 1982, p. 97)

"During his nineteen years imprisonment he had not shed a tear" (Hugo, [1862] 1982, p. 102).

One night, shortly after Valjean's release from prison, he stayed with the Bishop of Digne. At three o'clock in the morning he awakened from a troubled sleep and connived to steal the bishop's silver right from the room where the bishop slept. With a cap in one hand and a metal spike in the other, he slithered toward the bishop's basket of silver. Placing his cap back on his head he snatched the basket, unloaded the silver into his knapsack and hustled off into the night. Probably inadvertently, he left behind two silver candlesticks that had been burning during dinner.

Not many hours after daybreak, three members of the French police apprehended Jean Valjean and brought him to the bishop's home. The bishop called out:

> So here you are! . . . I'm delighted to see you. Had you forgotten that I gave you the candlesticks as well? They're silver like the rest, and worth a good two hundred francs. Did you forget to take them? . . . Go in peace. Incidentally, my friend, when next you come here you need not go through the garden. This door is never locked. . . . Do not forget, do not ever forget, that you have promised me to use the money to make yourself an honest man. (Hugo, [1862] 1982, pp. 110-111)

After this incident, Jean Valjean reconnected with his freedom and fled from town. But it was during this time in his life that

> He had moments of strange tenderness which he resisted with all the hardness of heart which twenty years had brought him. His state of mind was physically exhausting. He perceived with dismay that the kind of dreadful calm instilled in him by injustice and misfortune had begun to crumble. (Hugo, [1862] 1982, p. 112)

It had begun to crumble because of the binding relationship with the potent Bishop of Digne and the never-locked door to the bishop's environment.

Valjean changes and becomes a hero in every sense of the definition we have earlier portrayed. He devotes his life to raising the orphaned girl, Cosette; he saves the life of the soldier in love with his daughter; he spares the life of the policeman obsessed with Valjean's own death. After the meeting with the bishop, "It . . . [is] no longer in his power to behave though the bishop had not spoken to him and touched his heart" (Hugo, [1862] 1982, p. 116).

The mission of the Bishop of Digne is clear.

Appendix A

CASTT Intake Information

Student Name _____
Date _____

SIGNIFICANT EVENTS

Early Childhood (0-6 years)
_____
_____
_____
_____
_____
_____
_____

Latency (7-12 years)
_____
_____
_____
_____
_____

Adolescence (13-18 years)
_____
_____
_____
_____

Student Name _____

Date _____

HISTORY OF ABUSE
(Including psychological maltreatment, neglect,
physical assault, and sexual assault.)

Description and extent:

_____
_____
_____
_____

By whom: _____
_____

Age at onset: _____

Frequency: _____
_____

Duration (period of time): _____
_____

Disclosure (when, to/by whom, results):

_____
_____
_____

Attributions:

_____
_____
_____
_____

Student Name _____
Date _____

CONTINUA OF ADAPTIVE RESPONSES
TO TRAUMATIC STRESS

1. Numbed Response—Alexithymia—High Suicide Risk

_____
_____
_____

2. Hypervigilance—24-Hour Mad Watch—Paranoia

_____
_____
_____

3. Hyperarousal—Hyperactivity—Out-of-Control Behavior

_____
_____
_____

4. Modified Replay—Actual Replay—Obsessive Reenactment

_____
_____
_____

5. Heightened Creativity—Creative Independence—Dissociation

_____
_____
_____

6. Early Emotional Separation from Adults—Physical Separation from Adults—Drug Dependence/Unsafe Sexual Behavior

_____
_____
_____

Student Name _____

Date _____

STUDENT DATA SHEET

Previous Therapy:

_____

_____

_____

_____

Hospitalizations:

_____

_____

_____

_____

Any Psychological Testing? (dates/where/results):

_____

_____

_____

_____

Public School:

_____

Grade: _____   Special Ed: _____

Academic Advisor/Contact Person:

_____

Other Personnel: _____

_____

Social Services Caseworker: _____

Probation Officer: _____

Guardian Ad Litem: _____

Other: _____

_____

Student Name _____

Date _____

ATTACHMENT HISTORY

Have you felt close to anyone in: (please name)

Young Childhood (0-6):

_____

_____

_____

Latency (7-12):

_____

_____

_____

Adolescence (13-18):

_____

_____

_____

GOALS

_____

_____

_____

_____

_____

_____

_____

_____

_____

_____

_____

Appendix B

A Troubled Voice

The following poetry was written by a bright gang member. One of the poems was written in jail. This boy has a horribly violent child abuse history. Today, the boy is living in the community, working full time, and leading a *nonviolent* lifestyle.

> Crease my skull with lightning pain
> I'll remain distant, you remain the same
> Lost the key to my mind
> Lock is gone, decayed with time
> Blistered souls, the dance of the dead
> I could forgive, but never again
> Faces smiling upon red slashed throats
> Silently I laugh at your cautious approach
> The other side judging my ability
> Your world is ravaged, run amuck with senility
> Forsee the end of humility
> My cause, my supremacy
> Hearts dismantled, have lost memory
> Mercy wasted on the weak
> Pain bestowed on the meek
> Chaos, now a way of life
> Love, living in strife
> Wreck upon me, wrecked upon me
> Countless apologies, never spoke truth
> Limit me, control just a waste of time
> Take another white in its prime
> My existence thrives at your discretion
> You remain a member with my protection
> Hours of therapy, just mind dissection
> My honor, your rejection.

* * *

I am the authority on violence
I am the authority on what you need
Consciousness, distort reality
You suffer emotional overload
Love, complex, legality
Your mind slowly corrodes
Better, lost my sanity
You want some one with personality
Religion, blatant sexuality
That's the way the cookie crumbles
That's how people stay humble
That's how you will tumble
Tell me your pain
I won't laugh in your face
Tell me your terror
I won't cause a rumor
Let's get together and f— on your hate
Screaming Cain, raising the dead
Pretending to be a true individual
Remaining one step ahead
Existence can be so pitiful
End to the darkness, I join reality
Condemned as a man who can think
You don't understand, you can't understand
Close your eyes and come to me
Let go of the world, deadly sexuality.

*   *   *

All things at peace now
   This war has ended
   Feelings were hurt
   Emotions are deadened.
Words are weapons, destroyed a life
   Anger, hate, and depression
   All these poisons, your God-given right.
Take what you will to the end of time
   Remember your wisdom, your strength
   Tempt not the suicide knife.

Lift this veil from my eyes
> Remove yourself as a cheap disguise
> I can't change how you feel, can't dwell in the shadows
> I can't cause the light, not change what was said.

I can't forgive
> Living on a rift
> Encompass the soldier, he fought for his life
> Do not trespass, 'tis not your war.

What about the players who are left to mourn
> F—, it's the new world
> F—, it's the new plan
> Does not involve me, does not involve you.

Involves all the spectators with nothing to do
> Screaming is heard, but there is no one source
> Hatred is so solid
> Solutions are part of the course.

Introduce the new rat in the maze
> You can all laugh and then look away.

This is one world, there is one soul
> You have nothing, that they took.

It's a silent reply, to a silent invitation
> SILENCE speaks so much louder than words
> Another promise is broken, well that's nothing new.

Re-evaluate, another soul that is lost
> Calculate your social cost.

Monster, oh Yeah the parental giants
> Here comes the stealthy reproach.

Divine light, let us speak of God
> A man to be feared, a man long gone.

The scourge, the demented, the deranged, the pity of strife
> We shall die so that they may live.

SOCIETY'S RESENTMENT
> My distant rebellion
> Violence, educate, I'll be turning away.
> For all your words that I can't understand
> It's the new world
> It's the new plan
> We have no names.

*   *   *

Never hesitation, staked my claim along time ago
At 19, I knew I'd never see my home
The hours casted shadows over me
Easy to say, sorry easy to regret
Locked away, caged like a predator
Smiling as I watched the weak be consumed
Laughed as the mourners wept
I sit quietly years spent in worthless contemplation
Eyes in my back, I never show hesitation
A murderous situation, with ruthless contemplation
Society is the competition, too insane to get a vote

The pounding of the silence drums in my ears
The howls of the damned we pretend not to hear
The power, the ultimate theft an attracting lure
Criminals, animals, convicts, easy to call, but not to understand
My mind was divided, but my intentions whole
All the people I used and all the people I hurt
They say that I should be ashamed
I ain't in therapy, I'm doing life
There is no sun in this world, there is no sky
There's just the wall holding the animals with nowhere to live
As Jesus died on the cross, the Romans laughed
Just like Jesus, I'm relentless in my cause.

*   *   *

Hell: The home of the forgotten, the wondering children with empty
eyes
    You can't see the end until it looms over your shoulder
    Death's dark shadow marks all men.
To strive for a cause that is beyond my grasp
    Is a pity to the lost.
Control the things that are uncontrollable
    Burn in hell is my curse to you.
Relive your pain a thousandfold
    Hate my food, sorrow my drink.
Each hardship you endure is pleasure
    Your crippling loss, is my ecstasy.
Let your fantasies take control of your reality
    I will take enjoyment from your death.

Appendix C

Advocacy

In the next several years, we are hoping to start an Adolescent Rights Campaign. It is of interest to review the names of some well-known advocacy groups and realize that the word "adolescent" is left out. Nationally, note the Children's Defense Fund. In Colorado, there is the Colorado Children's Campaign and a Children's Legal Clinic. Teenagers have specific needs that can be successfully addressed in national and state agendas. It is time to separate their needs from the needs of young children.

A second advocacy vision of ours is to recognize young people who have experienced the trauma of abuse as heroes. Taking a national perspective, one of the duties of the president, as commander-in-chief, is to keep the strength of the country. A way in which the president accomplishes this mission is to award medals as decorations for bravery, for extraordinary achievement, and for acts of courage and heroism (e.g., the Purple Heart, to soldiers wounded in action; the Bronze Star, for heroism or achievement in military operations). Thus, another way of keeping the country strong might be to have an award or badge that would validate the gallantry, suffering, and heroism of children and adolescents who have endured child abuse.

The ritual of awarding a badge of courage could:

- bolster the self-esteem of a young person who has had his or her civil rights violated;
- validate the suffering endured;
- legitimize the courage shown;
- reframe the role of victim to one of strength; and
- neutralize the sense of betrayal and alienation.

Finally, when a youth is given the award, he or she could be asked to take an Oath of Responsibility to be an ambassador for preserving the safety and civil rights of other children and adolescents, and to join the Adolescent Rights Campaign.

Appendix D

Goals for Child Recovery from Traumatic Stress: A CASTT Model

1. Develop a sense of safety from significant adults who concretely provide safety through setting consistent limits and a predictable, soothing, energetic, and nurturing environment.
2. Develop trust—build close, meaningful relationships. Anchor and/or reanchor with significant adults.
3. Listen to adult teachers to redo developmental tasks. These tasks may include social skills development, emotional management, body boundary management, and academic skills development. Listening may mean learning from repetitive correctives.
4. Participate in activities that enable one to enjoy rewarding relationships, learn teamwork, and master specific skills, such as music, sports, painting, and writing.
5. Grieve losses and disappointments—develop ability to name different emotions and share emotions with significant adults.
6. Reframe environment as safe, nurturing, and supportive.
7. View self as brave and able to overcome hardships.
8. Let hopeful dreams become a part of one's worldview.

Note that the key difference between Adolescent Recovery and Child Recovery is the shift in the locus of control. With adolescents, recovery is collaborated in all stages. With children, the locus of control must be external–adults must take charge and provide the environment, the relationships, and the education for recovery.

This model represents the beginning work of the authors to develop a more specific model for children around the ages of six to twelve years old.

Appendix E

CASTT Information Sheet

Many young people have recovered from the terror of child abuse—however, recovery is difficult. Child abuse is traumatic by definition. It is a betrayal of the core expectation to be safely cared for by adults. Post-traumatic responses are often adaptive reactions to circumstances that should not occur.

In adolescence, some post-traumatic responses can be extreme. Teenagers, very much like skiers challenging extreme conditions, jeopardize safety. Survival is basic. Each child and each adolescent handles stress differently.

Factors that play into the degree of suffering from stress are:

1. Degree of emotional closeness to the abuser(s) (e.g., relative, close friend, adult in a position of trust);
2. Degree of physical closeness to abusive people (e.g., living in the same house, going to the same school);
3. Duration of abuse. If child abuse occurs over a long period of time, it can have a painful cumulative effect. It can corrupt moral development, erode emotional and physical health, and influence delays in developing academic skills. Brain neuro-transmission and structure can be altered;
4. Immediacy and competency of support system.

CASTT can be collapsed into three essential missions:

1. We must recognize suffering. Nelson Mandela, in his speech at the swearing in of the Truth and Reconciliation Commission in Capetown, South Africa, February 13, 1996, said, "It's necessary to identify those who have suffered."

This information sheet may be copied for use by teens, caretakers, and professionals.

2. We must provide hope and optimism. Over and over again, young people say that they need to hear that they are strong enough to come to terms with child abuse.
3. We must validate heroism. If not, we will continue to foster tragic heroes. Hamlet's words from Shakespeare's play attest to the dilemma of many young people: "To be, or not to be, that is the question:/Whether 'tis nobler in the mind to suffer/ The slings and arrows of outrageous fortune/Or to take arms against a sea of troubles/And by opposing end them" (Shakespeare, [c. 1601] 1988, p. 64).

Some universal signs of traumatic stress occur in the following categories:

Emotional

anger
fear
irritability
depression
anxiety
denial
panic
numbness

Behavioral

withdrawal
delinquency
hyperarousal
aggressive behavior
lethargic behavior
erratic behavior

Physical

stomach aches
headaches
fatigue
rapid heart rate
breathing difficulties
insomnia
eating problems
changes in brain functioning

Cognitive

confusion
hypervigilance
intrusive images
attention problems
concentration problems
memory problems
nightmares

Stress management tips for adults caring for children and adolescents who have been traumatized by child abuse:

1. Recognize suffering. Always tell young people you are sorry they had to endure child abuse and that you wish to help.
2. Give hope.

3. Validate bravery.
4. Keep safe—earn trust.
5. Listen.
6. Help children and adolescents regulate their emotions.
7. Nurture; give extra attention.
8. Keep track of youths. These young people need consistent caring throughout their lifetimes in order to neutralize the former lack of caring.
9. Help young people keep busy and help structure their time.
10. Do not take misbehavior personally.

Stress management tips for children (approximate ages six to twelve):

1. Play; balance suffering with fun.
2. Hug a trustworthy adult and your favorite stuffed animal each day.
3. Try hard to be kind to others even though others have been mean to you.
4. Do not be afraid to talk about suffering. Other children have suffered too.
5. Learn that you are not to blame. All children deserve to be protected from child abuse.
6. Learn that you have been courageous and brave to survive child abuse.
7. Do not copy corrupt, abusive behavior.
8. Eat well.
9. Keep rested.
10. Work hard in school.

Stress management tips for teenagers:

1. Keep yourself safe, and keep those around you safe.
2. Eat nutritious foods.
3. Speak with school staff when you are going through a rough time.
4. Exercise regularly.
5. Do not drink or use illegal drugs.
6. Learn to share your story without shame. Try not to numb your feelings.

Bibliography

Ainsworth, M.D.S., and Witting, B.A. (1969). Attachment and exploratory behavior of one-year-olds in a strange situation. In B.M. Foss (Ed.), *Determinants of infant behavior*, volume 4. London: Methuen.

American heritage dictionary of the English language. (1981). Revised edition. Boston: Houghton Mifflin Company.

American Humane Association: Children's Division. (1994). *Family Preservation*. Fact Sheet 11.

American Humane Association: Children's Division. (1995). *Child Abuse and Neglect Data*. Fact Sheet 1.

American Psychiatric Association. (1987). *Diagnostic and statistical manual of mental disorders*, third edition, revised. Washington, DC: American Psychiatric Association.

American Psychiatric Association. (1994). *Diagnostic and statistical manual of mental disorders,* fourth edition. Washington, DC: American Psychiatric Association.

Amole, T. (1991, May 6). Minorities jailed more often. *Rocky Mountain News, 7.*

Asen, K., George, E., Piper, R., and Stevens, A. (1989). A systems approach to child abuse: Management and treatment issues. *Child Abuse and Neglect, 13,* 45-57.

Banfield, E.C. (1990). *The unheavenly city revisited.* Prospect Heights, IL: Waveland Press, Inc.

Bell, S.M. (1970). The development of the concept of object as related to infant-mother attachment. *Child Development, 41,* 291-311.

Berliner, D.C., and Biddle, B.J. (1995). *The manufactured crisis: Myths, fraud and the attack on America's public schools.* Reading, MA: Addison-Wesley Publishing Company, Inc.

Bernard, T.J. (1992). *The cycle of juvenile justice.* New York: Oxford University Press.

Bertocci, D., and Schechter, M.D. (1991). Adopted adults' perception of their need to search: Implications for clinical practice. *Smith College Studies in Social Work, 61*(2), 179-196.

Born on the Fourth of July [film] (1989). Director and producer: O. Stone. Distributor: UP/Ixtian.

Bowlby, J. (1969). *Attachment and loss,* volume 1. New York: Basic Books.

Bowlby, J. (1973). *Attachment and loss,* volume 2. New York: Basic Books.

Boyd-Franklin, N. (1989). *Black families in therapy.* New York: The Guilford Press.

Briere, J.N. (1989). *Therapy for adults molested as children: Beyond survival.* New York: Springer Publishing Company.

Briere, J.N. (1992). *Child abuse trauma: Theory and treatment of the lasting effects.* Newbury Park: Sage Publications.

Briere, J.N., and Runtz, M. (1987). Post sexual abuse trauma. *Journal of Interpersonal Violence, 2*, 367-379.

Brown v. Board of Education of Topeka. (1954). 347 U.S. 483.

Bruner, J.S. (1960). *The process of education.* New York: Vintage Books.

Burgess, A.W., Groth, N.A., Holmstrom, L.L., and Sgroi, S.M. (1978). *Sexual assault of children.* Lexington, MA: D.C. Heath and Company.

Campbell, J. (with B. Moyers) (1988). *The power of myth.* New York: Doubleday.

Capitman, W. (1963). *Everyone's legal advisor.* New York: Gilbert Press, Inc.

Chapman, T. (1992). "Bang Bang Bang." On *Matters of the Heart* [CD] Elektra.

Children's Defense Fund. (1996, December). Juvenile violence decreasing: Fewer guns, more community involvement keeping children safe. *Children's Defense Fund Reports, 18*(1), 2.

Cicchetti, D., and Carlson, V. (Eds.) (1989). *Child maltreatment: Theory and research on the causes and consequences of child abuse and neglect.* Cambridge, England: Cambridge University Press.

Clark, K.B. (1965). *Dark ghetto: Dilemmas of social power.* New York: Harper and Row Publishers.

Colorado Children's Campaign. (1994). *KidsCount in Colorado 1994.* National KidsCount Project, funded by the Annie E. Casey Foundation.

Conrad, J. ([1902] 1984). *Youth; Heart of darkness; The end of the tether.* New York: Oxford University Press.

Damon, W. (1995). *Greater expectations.* New York: The Free Press.

Davis, S.M. (1974). *Rights of juveniles: The juvenile justice system.* New York: Clark Broadman Company, Ltd.

Donnelly, S. B. (1992, June 22). The fire around the Ice. *Time, 139,* 66-68.

Dryfoos, J.G. (1994). *Full-service schools: A revolution in health and social services for children, youth and families.* San Francisco: Jossey-Bass Publishers.

Easton, E.B. (1991). *Child protection report letter.* The Independent News Service for Professionals Working with Children and Youth.

Epstein, J. (pseud: Aristides) (1991, Summer). Knocking on three, Winston. *The American Scholar,* 327-336.

Erikson, E.H. (1950). *Childhood and society,* second edition. New York: W.W. Norton and Company, Inc.

Etzioni, A. (1993). *The spirit of the community: The reinvention of American society.* New York: Touchstone.

Freud, A. (1966). *The writings of Anna Freud volume II: The ego and the mechanisms of defense,* revised edition. New York: International Universities Press, Inc.

Gans, H.J. (1962). *The urban villagers: Group and class in the life of Italian-Americans.* New York: The Free Press.

Garbarino, J., Guttman, E., and Seeley, J.W. (1986). *The psychologically battered child: Strategies for identification, assessment, and intervention.* San Francisco: Jossey-Bass Publishers.

Gardner, H. (1993). *Multiple intelligences: The theory in practice.* New York: Basic Books.

Gelles, R. (1996). *The book of David: How preserving families can cost children's lives.* New York: Basic Books.

Gibbs, N. (1995, July 3) Working harder, getting nowhere. *Time, 139,* 17-20.

Ginsburg, H., and Opper, S. (1969). *Piaget's theory of intellectual development: An introduction.* New Jersey: Prentice Hall, Inc.

Ginzberg, E., Berliner, H.S., and Ostow, M. (1988). *Young people at risk: Is prevention possible?* Boulder, CO: Westview Press.

Gordon, M.M. (1963). *Social class in American sociology.* New York: McGraw-Hill Book Company, Inc.

Hammersmith, S.K. (1987). A sociological approach to counseling homosexual clients and their families. *Journal of Homosexuality, 14*(1/2), 173-190.

Hapgood, H. (1967). *The spirit of the ghetto.* Cambridge, MA: The Belknap Press of Harvard University Press.

Helfer, R.E., and Kempe, R.S. (Eds.) (1987). *The battered child,* fourth edition, revised. Chicago: The University of Chicago Press.

Hetrick, E.S., and Martin, A.D. (1987). Developmental issues and their resolution for gay and lesbian adolescents. *Journal of Homosexuality, 14,* (1/2), 2543.

Higham, J. (1988). *Strangers in the land: Patterns of American nativism 1860-1925.* New Brunswick, NJ: Rutgers University Press.

Holloran, P.C. (1989). *Boston's wayward children: Social services for homeless children 1830-1930.* Cranbury, NJ: Fairleigh Dickinson University Press.

Holt, J. (1969). *The underachieving school.* New York: Dell Publishing Co., Inc.

Hugo, V. ([1862] 1982). *Les misérables* (N. Denny, Trans). London, England: Penguin Books.

Hunter, J., and Schaecher, R. (1987). Stresses on lesbian and gay adolescents in schools. *Social Work in Education, 9,* 180-190.

Ingraham v. Wright (1977). 97S Ct 1401; 430 US 651; 51 Led 2nd 711.

Ingrassia, M., and McCormick, J. (1994, April 25). Why leave children with bad parents? *Newsweek, 123,* 52-58.

James, W. ([1890] 1983). *The principles of psychology.* Cambridge, MA: Harvard University Press.

Janet, P. (1924). *Principles of psychotherapy.* New York: The Macmillian Company.

Jordan, J.V. (1989). Relational development: Therapeutic implications of empathy and shame. *Work in Progress No. 39.* Wellesley, MA: Stone Center, Wellesley College.

Jordan, J.V., Surrey, J.L., and Kaplan, A.G. (1982). Women and empathy. *Work in Progress No. 2.* Wellesley, MA: The Stone Center Working Papers Series.

Kempe, C.H., Silverman, F.N., Steele, B.F., Droegemueller, S.H., and Silver, H.K. (1962). The battered child syndrome. *Journal of the American Medical Association, 181,* 17-24.

Kiell, N. (Ed.) (1964). *The universal experience of adolescence.* New York: International Universities Press.

Kinsler, F. (1990a). Post-traumatic stress disorder: Generations of the Holocaust. Presented at The Ruth Hutton Fred Annual Lecture, Baylor College of Medicine, May 2.

Kinsler, F. (1990b). Groups to heal old wounds of war. Presented at International Society for Traumatic Stress Studies, New Orleans, October 28-31.

Kirschner, D., and Nagel, L.S. (1988). Antisocial behavior in adoptees: Patterns and dynamics. *Child and Adolescent Social Work Journal, 5*(4), 300-314.

Knowles, J. (1963). *A separate peace.* New York: Dell.

Kozol, J. (1991). *Savage inequalities: Children in America's schools.* New York: Crown Publishers, Inc.

Krystal, H. (1978). Trauma and affects. *Psychoanalytic Study of the Child, 33,* 81-116.

Lazarus, E. (1883). The new colossus. In *Catalog of the Pedestal Fund Art Loan Exhibition.* New York: National Academy of Design, 9.

LeVine, E.S., and Sallee, A. L. (1990). Critical phases among adoptees and their families: Implications for therapy. *Child and Adolescent Social Work Journal, 7*(3), 217-232.

Levine, M., and Levine, A. (1992). *Helping children: A social history.* New York: Oxford University Press.

Lewis, D.O., Mallouh, C., and Webb, V. (1989). Child abuse, delinquency, and violent criminality. In D. Cicchetti and V. Carlson (Eds.), *Child maltreatment: Theory and research on the causes and consequences of child abuse and neglect* (707-721). Cambridge, England: Cambridge University Press.

Lewis, D.O., Pincus, J.H., Feldman, M., Jackson, L., and Bard, B. (1986). Psychiatric, neurological, and psychoeducational characteristics of 15 death row inmates in the United States. *American Journal of Psychiatry, 143*(7), 838-845.

Lipsher, S. (1993, March 6). Juvenile defenders to be sent out of state. *The Denver Post,* 4B.

Long. M.J., and Chapman, R. (1996). *Handbook of rights to special education in Colorado: A guide for parents.* Denver: The Legal Center.

MacNeil/Lehrer News Hour (1994, June 15). Executive producer: L. Crystal. New York and Washington, DC: Public Broadcasting Service.

Martin, A.D., and Hetrick, E.S. (1988). The stigmatization of the gay and lesbian adolescent. *Journal of Homosexuality, 15*(1/2), 163-183.

Maslow, A. (1968). *Toward a psychology of being.* New York: Van Nostrand Reinhold.

Mayer, J. (1995, June 5). Rejecting Gina. *The New Yorker,* 43-51.

McCann, I.L., and Pearlman, L.A. (1990). *Psychological trauma and the adult survivor: Theory, therapy and transformation.* New York: Brunner/Mazel.

Menninger, K.A. (1966). *The crime of punishment.* New York: The Viking Press.

Morson, B. (1992, January 31). The impossible dream? *Rocky Mountain News,* 8.

Myers, L. (1995, September 8). Juvenile arrest rate on a tear. *Rocky Mountain News,* 2A.

National Advisory Mental Health Council (1993). Health care reform for Americans with severe mental illnesses: Report of the National Advisory Mental Health Council. *American Journal of Psychiatry, 150*(10), 1447-1465.

New Yorker, The. (1993, September 13). Cover photo.

Nietzsche, F. (1973). *Beyond good and evil: Prelude to a philosophy of the future* (R.J. Hollingdale, Trans.). Middlesex, England: Penguin Books.

Ordinary People [film] (1980). Director: R. Redford. Distribution: Paramount.

Partridge, P.C. (1991). The particular challenges of being adopted. *Smith College Studies in Social Work, 61*(2), 197-208.

Perez, C.M., and Widom, C.S. (1994). Childhood victimization and long-term intellectual and academic outcomes. *Child Abuse and Neglect, 18*(8), 617-633.

Perry, B.D. (1993a). Neuro-development and the neuro-physiology of trauma I: Conceptual considerations for clinical work with maltreated children. *The Advisor: American Professional Society on the Abuse of Children, 6*(1) Spring, 193-199.

Perry, B.D. (1993b). Neuro-development and neuro-physiology of trauma II: Clinical work along the alarm-fear-terror continuum. *The Advisor: American Professional Society on the Abuse of Children, 6*(2) Summer, 200-207.

Perry, B.D. (1996, April). The Rosenberry Conference, The Arvada Center for the Arts and Humanities, Arvada, CO: Children's Hospital.

Plessy v. Ferguson. (1896). 16 S Ct 1138; 163 US 537; 41 Led 256.

Polier, J. W. (1989). *Juvenile justice in double jeopardy: The distanced community and vengeful retribution.* Hillsdale, NJ: Lawrence Erlbaum Associates, Publishers.

Prescott, P.S. (1981). *The child savers: Juvenile justice observed.* New York: Alfred A. Knopf.

Ravitch, D. (1983). *The troubled crusade: American education, 1945-1980.* New York: Basic Books, Inc.

Reik, T. (1949). *Listening with the third ear: The inner experience of a psychoanalyst.* New York: Farrar, Straus and Company.

Riley, M. (1992, January 27). *Time.* "Corridors of agony." 48-55.

Rocky Mountain News (1991, December 27). "Juvenile violence surges in Colorado: Murder, assault arrests increase dramatically since mid-80s in state and U.S. officials fear there is no end in sight." 1A.

Rocky Mountain News (1992, January 31). "21% of the class of 1991 quit." 1A.

Rocky Mountain News (1992, June 6). "Black teen jobless rate drops 50%." (Reuters Newswire Service). 59.

Rocky Mountain News (1993, February 6). "House passes two bad-kids bills." 26.

Rocky Mountain News (1993, September 8). "We've got to change: Romer pleads for laws to disarm kids, takes shots at NRA as special session opens." 1A.

Rocky Mountain News (1993, September 9). "House toughens gun bill: Laws would slap kids with felony, 5 days in jail for illegally having guns." 1A.

Rocky Mountain News (1997, February 7). "U.S. tops in child murders." (Reuter's Newswire Service). 3A.

Rubin, H.T. (1985). *Behind the black robes: Juvenile court judges and the court.* Beverly Hills, CA: Sage Publications.

Rutter, M., Maugham, B., Mortimer, P., and Ouston, J. (with A. Smith) (1979). *Fifteen thousand hours: Secondary schools and their effects on children.* Cambridge, MA: Harvard University Press.

Ryan, C. (1966). *The last battle.* New York: Fawcett Popular Library.

Safer, M. (1992, June 28). "Epidemic: Violence in the lives of young people." *60 Minutes* ([TV broadcast] Creator and Executive Producer: D. Hewitt). Columbia Broadcasting System.

Saunders, J.M., and Valente, S.M. (1987). Suicide risk among gay men and lesbians: A review. *Death Studies, 11,* 1-23.

Schorr, L.B. (with D. Schorr) (1989). *Within our reach: Breaking the cycle of disadvantage.* New York: Anchor Books, Doubleday.

Schwartz, I.M. (1989). *(In)Justice for juveniles: Rethinking the best interests of the child.* Lexington, MA: Lexington Books, D.C. Heath and Company.

Seaberg, J.R., and Tolley, E.S. (1986, Fall). Predictors of the length of stay in foster care. *Social Work Research and Abstracts,* 11-17.

Shakespeare, W. [c. 1601] (1988). *Hamlet.* (D. Bevington, Ed.). Toronto: Bantam Books.

Shyne, A.W., and Schroeder, A.G. (1978). *National study of social services to children and their families.* Washington, DC: U.S. Department of Health, Education and Welfare, National Center for Child Advocacy.

Shulman, S. (1997). *KidsCount in Colorado 1997.* Colorado Children's Campaign, National KidsCount Project, funded by the Annie E. Casey Foundation.

Simon, R.D., and Simon, D.K. (1982). The effect of foster parent selection and training on service delivery. *Child Welfare League of America, LXI* (8), 515-524.

Smart, M.S., and Smart, R.C. (1967). *Children: Development and relationships.* New York: The Macmillan Company.

Smith, D. (1986, May 29). Bond unites children of Holocaust. *Los Angeles Times,* 1.

Steele, S. (1990). *The content of our character: A new vision of race in America.* New York: Harper Collins Publishers.

Steiner, H., Garcia, I.G., and Matthews, Z. (1997, March). Posttraumatic stress disorder in incarcerated juvenile delinquents. *Journal of the American Academy of Child and Adolescent Psychiatry, 36*(3), 357-365.

Subhumans. (1983). "Mickey Mouse Is Dead." On *The Day the Country Died* [album]. Bluurg.

Taylor, G.J. (1989). Alexithymia. *The Harvard Medical School Mental Health Letter, 5*(12), 6.

Thomas, P. (1996, December 16-22). Advocate, counselor and judge: In juvenile court, there are no easy answers when it comes to deciding a child's future. *The Washington Post National Weekly Edition,* 6.

Time (1993, August 2). "Big shots: An inside look at the deadly love affair between America's kids and their guns." Cover headline.

Tizard, J., and Tizard, B. (1971). The social development of two-year-old children in residential nurseries. In: H. R. Schalfer (Ed.), *The origins of human social relations.* London and New York: Academic Press, 147-163.

Toch, T. (1991). *In the name of excellence: The struggle to reform the nation's schools, why it's failing, and what should be done.* Oxford: Oxford University Press.

van der Kolk, B.A. (1985). Adolescent vulnerability to post traumatic stress disorder. *Psychiatry, 48,* 365-370.

van der Kolk, B.A. (1987). *Psychological trauma.* Washington, DC: American Psychiatric Press.

van der Kolk, B.A. (1988). The trauma spectrum: The interaction of biological and social events in the genesis of the trauma response. *Journal of Traumatic Stress, 1,* 273-290.

van der Kolk, B.A. (1989). The compulsion to repeat the trauma. *Psychiatric Clinics of North America, 12,* 389-411.

van der Kolk, B.A. (1991, July 29-August 2). Harvard Seminar, Cape Cod, MA.

van der Kolk, B.A., Perry, J.C., and Herman, J.L. (1991). Childhood origins of self-destructive behavior. *American Journal of Psychiatry, 148,* 1665-1671.

van der Kolk, B.A., and van der Hart, O. (1989). Pierre Janet and the breakdown of adaptation in psychological trauma. *American Journal of Psychiatry, 146,* 1530-1539.

VerMeulen, M. (1992, June 21). "What people earn." *Parade Magazine,* 5.

Warer, W., Lloyd, M.M., and Eells, K. (1949). *Social class in America: A manual of procedure for the measurement of social status.* Chicago: Science Research Associates, Inc.

Widom, C.S. (1994). Childhood victimization and adolescent problem behaviors. In R.D. Ketterlinus and M.E. Lamb (Eds.), *Adolescent problem behaviors: Issues and research* (127-164). Hillsdale, New Jersey: Lawrence Erlbaum Associates.

Wilcox, D. (1989). "Eye of the Hurricane." On *How Did You Find Me Here?* [CD]. A&M Records.

Winnicott, D. W. (1965). *The maturational processes and the facilitating environment: Studies in the theory of emotional development.* Madison: International Universities Press, Inc.

Zigler, E., and Hall, N. W. (1989). Physical child abuse in America: Past, present and future. In D. Cicchetti and V. Carlson (Eds.), *Child maltreatment.* Cambridge, England: Cambridge University Press.

Suggested Readings

Anthony, E.J., and Cohler, B.J. (Eds.) (1987). *The invulnerable child.* New York: The Guilford Press.

Berland, D.I., Homlish, J.S., and Blotcky, M.J. (1989). Adolescent gangs in the hospital. Paper presented at annual meeting of the American Academy of Child and Adolescent Psychiatry, October 1982. The Menninger Foundation.

Bernheimer, C., and Kahane, C. (Eds.) (1985). In *Dora's case: Freud-hysteria-feminism.* New York: Columbia University Press.

Bowen, M. (1978). *Family therapy in clinical practice.* New York: Jason Aronson, Inc.

Bowman, B. (1986). Early experiential environment, maternal bonding and the susceptibility to post traumatic stress disorder. *Military Medicine, 151,* 528-531.

Briere, J.N. (1996). *Therapy for adults molested as children: Beyond survival* (Second edition). New York: Springer Publishing Company, Inc.

Brill, A.A. (Ed.) (1938). *The basic writings of Sigmund Freud.* New York: The Modern Library.

Cleckley, H. (1982). *The mask of sanity.* New York: New American Library.

Crane, S. (1951). *The red badge of courage.* New York: Random House.

Daly, C.U. (Ed.) (1968). *The quality of inequality: Urban and suburban schools.* Chicago: The University of Chicago Center for Policy Study.

Donovan, D.M., and McIntyre, D. (1990). *Healing the hurt child: A developmental contextual approach.* New York: W.W. Norton and Company.

Elkind, D. (1974). *Children and adolescents: Interpretive essays on Jean Piaget* (Second edition). New York: Oxford University Press.

Elkind, D. (1984). *All grown up and no place to go: Teenagers in crisis.* Reading, MA: Addison-Wesley.

Esman, A.H. (Ed.) (1975). *The psychology of adolescence: Essential readings.* New York: International University Press, Inc.

Eth, S., and Pynoos, R.S. (Eds.) (1985). *Post traumatic stress disorder in children.* Washington, DC: American Psychiatric Press, Inc.

Fauber, R.L., and Long, N. (1991). Children in context: The role of the family in child psychotherapy. *Journal of Consulting and Clinical Psychology, 59,* 813-820.

Feldman, L.B. (1988). Integrating individual and family therapy in the treatment of symptomatic children and adolescents. *American Journal of Psychotherapy, XLII,* 272-280.

Finkelhor, D. (1984). *Child sexual abuse: New theory and research.* New York: The Free Press.

Firestone, W.A., and Drews, D.H. (1987). The Coordination of Education and Social Services, Early Intervention, Substance Abuse, and Teen Pregnancy Programs. Philadelphia, PA: Research for Better Schools, (215)574-9300, thirty-one page booklet.

Fishman, C.H. (1988). *Treating troubled adolescents: A family therapy approach.* New York: Basic Books, Inc.

Forer, L.G. (1994). *A rage to punish: The unintended consequences of mandatory sentencing.* New York: W.W. Norton and Company.

Fraiberg, S.H. (1959). *The magic years: Understanding and handling the problems of early childhood.* New York: Charles Scribner's Sons.

Frankl, V.E. (1967). *Psychotherapy and existentialism: Selected papers on logotherapy.* New York: Clarion.

Freud, S. (1901). *The complete psychological works of Sigmund Freud: Psychopathology of everyday life, volume VI.* London: The Hogarth Press Limited.

Freud, S. (1955). *The complete psychological works of Sigmund Freud: Studies on hysteria, volume II (1893-1895).* London: The Hogarth Press Limited.

Freud, S. (1962). *The complete psychological works of Sigmund Freud: Early psychoanalytic publications, volume III (1893-1899).* London: The Hogarth Press Limited.

Freud, S. (1966). *The complete psychological works of Sigmund Freud: Prepsychoanalytic publications and unpublished drafts, volume I (1886-1899).* London: The Hogarth Press Limited.

Garbarino, J., Dubrow, N., Kostelny, K., and Pardo, C. (1992). *Children in danger: Coping with the consequences of community violence.* San Francisco: Jossey-Bass Publishers.

Gil, E. (1988). *Treatment of adult survivors of childhood abuse.* Walnut Creek, CA: Launch Press.

Gil, E., and Johnson, T.C. (1993). *Sexualized children: Assessment and treatment of sexualized children and children who molest.* Rockville, MD: Launch Press.

Goldstein, J., Freud, A., and Solnit, A.J. (1979). *Beyond the best interests of the child* (Rev. ed.). New York: The Free Press.

Goodwin, J. (1988). Post traumatic symptoms in abused children. *Journal of Traumatic Stress, 1,* 475-488.

Haynes-Seman, C., and Baumgarten, D. (1994). *Children speak for themselves: Using the Kempe interactional assessment to evaluate allegations of parent-child sexual abuse.* New York: Brunner/Mazel.

Herman, J.L. (with L. Kirschman) (1981). *Father-daughter incest.* Cambridge, MA: Harvard University Press.

Herman, J.L. (1992). *Trauma and recovery.* New York: Basic Books.

Herman, J.L., Perry, J.C., and van der Kolk, B.A. (1989). Childhood trauma in borderline personality disorder. *American Journal of Psychiatry, 146,* 490-495.

Horowitz, M.J. (1986). *Stress response syndromes* (Second edition). Northvale, NJ: Jason Aronson, Inc.

Horowitz, M.J., Wilner, N., and Alvarez, W. (1979). Impact of event scale: A measure of subjective stress. *Psychosomatic Medicine, 41,* 209-218.

Jacobson, A., and Charaine, H. (1990). The relevance of childhood sexual abuse to adult psychiatric inpatient care. *Hospital and Community Psychiatry, 41,* 54-158.

James, B. (1989). Treating traumatized children: New insights and creative interventions. Lexington, MA: D.C. Heath and Company.

James, B. (1994). *Handbook for treatment of attachment-trauma problems in children.* Lexington, MA: Macmillian Company.

Johnson, D.R. (1987). Perspective: The role of the creative arts therapies in diagnosis and treatment of psychological trauma. *The Arts in Psychotherapy, 14,* 7-13.

Kaplan, H.I., and Sadock, B.J. (Eds.) (1995). *Comprehensive textbook of psychiatry* (Sixth edition, Vols. 1-2). Baltimore, MD: Williams and Wilkins.

Kardiner, A. (1941). *The traumatic neuroses of war.* New York: P.B. Hoeber, Inc.

Karen, R. (1994). *Becoming attached: Unfolding the mystery of the infant-mother bond and its impact on later life.* New York: Warner Books, Inc.

Kazdin, A. (1991). Effectiveness of psychotherapy with children and adolescents. *Journal of Consulting and Clinical Psychology, 59*(6), 785-798.

Kendall, P.C. and Morris, R.J. (1991). Child therapy: Issues and recommendations. *Journal of Consulting and Clinical Psychology, 59*(6), 777-784.

Kinard, E.M. (1979). The psychological consequences of abuse for the child. *Journal of Social Issues, 35,* 82-99.

Kohl, H. (1967). *36 children.* New York: Plume, Penguin Books.

Kübler-Ross, E. (1969). *On death and dying.* New York: Macmillian.

Lewis, A. (1964). *New York Times: Portrait of a decade.* New York: Random House.

Lindholm, T., Lehtinen, V., Hyyppa, M.T., and Puukka, P. (1990). Alexithymic features in relation to the dexamethasone suppression test in a Finnish population sample. *American Journal of Psychiatry, 147*(9), 1216-1219.

Lyons, J.A. (1987). Post traumatic stress disorder in children and adolescents: A review of the literature. *Journal of Developmental and Behavioral Pediatrics, 8, 349-356.*

Mahler, M.S., Pine, F., and Bergman, A. (1975). *The psychological birth of the human infant.* New York: Basic Books, Inc.

Malmquist, C.P. (1986). Children who witness parental murder: Posttraumatic aspects. *Journal of the American Academy of Child Psychiatry, 25*(3), 320-325.

Martin, J.A. (1989). The comparative effects of three treatment methods on adolescent runaway behavior. *Dissertation Abstracts International, 50,* 2158-B.

Mauzerall, H. (1983). Emancipation from foster care: The independent living project. *Child Welfare, LXII*(1), 47-53.

McFarlane, A.C. (1987). Posttraumatic phenomena in a longitudinal study of children following a natural disaster. *American Academy of Child and Adolescent Psychiatry, 5,* 764-769.

Menninger, K.A. (1931). *The human mind.* New York: F.S. Crofts and Company.

Minuchin, S. (1974). *Families and family therapy.* Cambridge, MA: Harvard University Press.

Myers, J.E.B. (Ed.) (1994). *The backlash: Child protection under fire.* Thousand Oaks, CA: Sage Publishers.

Ochberg, F.M. (Ed.) (1988). *Post-traumatic therapy and victims of violence.* New York: Brunner/Mazel, Inc.

Oliver, J.M., Searight, R., and Lightfoot, S. (1988). Client characteristics as determinants of intervention modality and therapy progress. *American Journal of Orthopsychiatry, 58,* 43-51.

Pitman, R.K. (1989). The psychobiology of the trauma response. Position paper for U.S. Government, Veterans Administration Medical Center. Manchester, NH, 1-24.

Previte, M.T. (1993). *Hungry ghosts: One woman's mission to save America's empty souls.* Grand Rapids, MI: Zondervan.

Pynoos, R.S., Calvin, F., Nader, K., Arroyo, W., Steinberg, A., Eth, S., Nunez, F., and Fairbanks, L. (1987). Life threat and Posttraumatic stress in school-age children. *Archives General Psychiatry, 44*(12), 1057-1063.

Sanford, L.T. (1990). *Strong at the broken places: Overcoming the trauma of childhood abuse.* New York: Random House.

Simos, B.G. (1979). *A time to grieve: Loss as a universal experience.* New York: Family Service Association of America.

Sonnenberg, S.M. (1988). Victims of violence and post traumatic stress disorder. *Psychiatric Clinics of North America, 11*(4), 581-590.

Stanley, A. (1990, June 18). "Child warriors." *Time, 135,* 30-52.

Steele, B.F. (1986). Notes on the lasting effects of early child abuse throughout the life cycle. *Child Abuse and Neglect, 10*(3), 283-291.

Stroup, H. (1986). *Social welfare pioneers.* Chicago: Nelson-Hall.

Taylor, G.J., Parker, J.D.A., and Bagby, M.R. (1990). A preliminary investigation of alexithymia in men with psychoactive substance dependence. *American Journal of Psychiatry, 147*(9), 1228-1230.

Terr, L.C. (1981). Psychic trauma in children: Observations following the Chowchilla school bus kidnapping. *American Journal of Psychiatry, 138*(1), 14-19.

Terr, L. (1990). *Too scared to cry: Psychic trauma in childhood.* New York: Harper and Row Publishers.

van der Kolk, B.A., McFarlane, A.C., and Weisaeth, L. (Eds.) (1996). *Traumatic stress: The effects of overwhelming experience on mind, body and society.* New York: The Guilford Press.

Watzlawick, P., Weakland, J., and Fisch, R. (1974). *Change: Principles of problem formation and problem resolution.* New York: W.W. Norton and Company.

Weissman, H.H. (1978). *Integrating services for troubled families.* San Francisco: Jossey-Bass.

Wollons, R. (Ed.). (1993). *Children at risk in America: History, concepts and public policy.* Albany, NY: State University of New York Press.

Index

Page numbers followed by the letter "i" indicate illustrations.

Order Your Own Copy of
This Important Book for Your Personal Library!

BRIDGING WORLDS
Understanding and Facilitating Adolescent Recovery from the Trauma of Abuse

_____ in hardbound at $39.95 (ISBN: 0-7890-0089-X)

_____ in softbound at $24.95 (ISBN: 0-7890-0227-2)

COST OF BOOKS_____

OUTSIDE USA/CANADA/
MEXICO: ADD 20%_____

POSTAGE & HANDLING_____
*(US: $3.00 for first book & $1.25
for each additional book)
Outside US: $4.75 for first book
& $1.75 for each additional book)*

SUBTOTAL_____

IN CANADA: ADD 7% GST_____

STATE TAX_____
*(NY, OH & MN residents, please
add appropriate local sales tax)*

FINAL TOTAL_____
*(If paying in Canadian funds,
convert using the current
exchange rate. UNESCO
coupons welcome.)*

☐ **BILL ME LATER:** ($5 service charge will be added)
(Bill-me option is good on US/Canada/Mexico orders only;
not good to jobbers, wholesalers, or subscription agencies.)

☐ Check here if billing address is different from
shipping address and attach purchase order and
billing address information.

Signature_____

☐ **PAYMENT ENCLOSED: $**_____

☐ **PLEASE CHARGE TO MY CREDIT CARD.**

☐ Visa ☐ MasterCard ☐ AmEx ☐ Discover
☐ Diner's Club

Account # _____

Exp. Date _____

Signature _____

Prices in US dollars and subject to change without notice.

NAME _____

INSTITUTION _____

ADDRESS _____

CITY _____

STATE/ZIP _____

COUNTRY _____ COUNTY (NY residents only) _____

TEL _____ FAX _____

E-MAIL_____

May we use your e-mail address for confirmations and other types of information? ☐ Yes ☐ No

Order From Your Local Bookstore or Directly From
The Haworth Press, Inc.
10 Alice Street, Binghamton, New York 13904-1580 • USA
TELEPHONE: 1-800-HAWORTH (1-800-429-6784) / Outside US/Canada: (607) 722-5857
FAX: 1-800-895-0582 / Outside US/Canada: (607) 772-6362
E-mail: getinfo@haworth.com
PLEASE PHOTOCOPY THIS FORM FOR YOUR PERSONAL USE.

BOF96